Black American Literature
Fiction

Edited by

Darwin T. Turner

North Carolina Agricultural and
Technical State University

Charles E. Merrill Publishing Company
A Bell & Howell Company
Columbus, Ohio

Standard Book Number: 675-09500-X

Library of Congress Catalog Number: 79-82446

1 2 3 4 5 6 7 8 9 10 11 12 — 76 75 74 73 72 71 70 69

Printed in the United States of America

To
my wife Jeanne
and
my children,
Pamela, Darwin Keith, and Rachon,
my present and my future

Preface

A word, perhaps, needs to be said about the title. When James Baldwin wrote, "Nobody knows my name," he could not have foreseen the violent dispute which would be incited a decade later by those who, rejecting the term "Negro," wish to be described as "black." The title of this volume indicates my awareness of and sympathy with that group even if I cannot totally agree with their argument.

The controversy is not trivial. It reflects a troubled, sometimes desperate search for identity by a people who have lived in a society which consciously stripped their racial identity from them. Originally, we were African, but we were taken from Africa. Voluntarily or involuntarily, we mixed with people of other nations and other races; but, as long as our skin remained dark and our features Negroid, we were identified as Negroes rather than as members of any other ethnic or political group. And, despite our three-century existence in America, we have never been recognized fully as Americans. Because of such a history, we have sought to retain or regain our identity and to proclaim that identity with a meaningful name.

Early in the twentieth century, the term "colored" linked the causes of the black American with other dark-skinned peoples of the world. To others, "Afro-American" seemed a more accurate description of our identity. Then, a solution seemed to lie in a crusade to capitalize "negro" and thus change it from a sometimes derogatory description to the name of a racially proud group. Now, rejecting "Negro" as a term which they identify with slavery and servility, many members of the group insist upon "black."

In this work I shall use "black" generally to contrast with "white" and most often to identify individuals of African ancestry who wrote in this country before the United States gained its identity as a nation. I shall also use "black" specifically to refer to writers identified with Black Nationalism or with the Black Arts Movement. Frequently, however, I shall use "black," "Afro-American," and "Negro" interchangeably. My reason — if I need one—is not that I am too old to change my habits but that I have struggled too diligently to discover my own identity to permit it to be dislodged by the mere question of whether I am called "Negro" or "black."

Let me take this opportunity to express a very deep appreciation to Mrs. Fannie Garrison and Mrs. Nina Bridges, who helped type this work, and to Miss Myrtle Howard, whose general assistance was invaluable. I wish also to express gratitude to my wife, Jeanne, who endured while I wrote.

Contents

Introduction

This book is a collection of short works by black Americans who have earned recognition as writers of fiction. The choice of selections is a major problem for any editor who proposes such a collection. Talented authors frequently abandon the short story form after they have published favorably received novels. Consequently, an editor who wishes to include short works from the best-known writers of fiction may be forced to select pieces which fail to exemplify the style and thought which characterize the more mature work of those authors. In some instances, in fact, the early work of a famous novelist may be inferior to stories of writers most familiar to contemporary readers were selected, cause most students need to become more familiar with the history of literature by black Americans, it seems more important to offer a collection of stories by the best-known writers than to prepare a collection of the best stories.

Even the term "best-known" must be qualified. If only the writers most familiar to contemporary readers were selected, the collection probably would be limited to those published during the past thirty years. To provide a reasonably representative picture of the literary achievements throughout the twentieth century, however, I have included works from the best-known writers of each decade. If it seems that too much space has been given to the early writers, the reason is my belief that, because works of the past decade are available in libraries and paperbacked books, it is important in an anthology to provide readers with selections which may be more difficult to obtain.

Despite these apologies for the uneven quality of the selections, I believe that this anthology provides models for the study of the short story as an art form and, simultaneously, provides representative materials for a history of short fiction by black writers.

The first Afro-American makers of fiction were the slaves who retold and adapted to the new world the tales which their fathers had brought from Africa. These were folk tales which no individual proclaimed to be his unique creation. Certainly, individuals invented them, but later narrators felt free to modify them; for these stories about heroes—animal and human—whose character traits were well known to the listeners were the product of the race. They reflected the imagination, the aspirations, and the ideals of the black men of America. And, because they were imaginative departures from Anglo-Saxon tradition, they became an important addition to American culture, as Joel Chandler Harris realized after the enthusiastic reception of the first volume of Uncle Remus tales.

Folk tales were circulated orally. The Afro-American's development as a *writer* of short stories, however, proceeded more slowly for a number of reasons. First, and most obvious, is the fact that relatively few slaves and freemen knew how to write; most Southern states forbade the education of black Americans. Second, the popular medium for the short story in America is the periodical, but few early nineteenth-century editors desired material written by Afro-Americans. Those few were abolitionists looking for "true," horrifying autobiographies to win converts to their cause.

Consequently, even though Afro-Americans repeated African tales in the seventeenth century and published poetry as early as 1760, the first serious short story writers did not appear until more than twenty years after the Emancipation Proclamation. In 1887, *The Atlantic Monthly* published Charles Waddell Chesnutt's "The Goophered Grapevine," the story of the conjuring or enchanting of a vineyard, told by a former slave who wants to prevent the sale of the vineyard. Although *The Atlantic* continued to publish Chesnutt's work, the editor, possibly fearing criticism or cancellation of subscriptions, avoided identifying the writer as Negro.

In contrast, the publishers of Paul Laurence Dunbar's stories wanted to identify him. By 1897, Dunbar had earned national fame as a poet, but he was still crude and inexperienced as a writer of fiction. Hoping to capitalize on his popularity, publishers not only accepted his stories but even collected them, in *Folks from Dixie* (1898), a year before the more experienced, more artistic Chesnutt could persuade anyone to accept *The Conjure Woman and Other Tales.*

The success of Dunbar and Chesnutt did not encourage boldness from publishers. Some Afro-Americans, such as James McGirt and

Fenton Johnson, published their own work; but black writers of short fiction remained unknown until the Harlem Renaissance.

The Harlem Renaissance is the name popularly assigned to that decade during which white Americans rediscovered the culture of black Americans. A combination of circumstances produced the Renaissance. First, white writers became interested in black people. In 1917, Ridgely Torrence issued *Three Plays for a Negro Theatre*, and four years later Eugene O'Neill wrote *The Emperor Jones*. For Afro-American readers, the four plays are limited because they concentrate on primitive aspects of Negro life and psychology; nevertheless, the four helped awaken artists to awareness of the Negro as subject for serious realistic presentation. Before the Twenties ended, the subject was explored significantly by such writers as Carl van Vechten (*Nigger Heaven*), Gertrude Stein (*Melanctha*), Waldo Frank (*Holiday*), Sherwood Anderson (*Dark Laughter*), William Faulkner (*The Sound and the Fury*), and Dubose Heyward (*Porgy* and *Mamba's Daughters*). A second cause of the Renaissance was the popularity of jazz. The post-war generation danced to a jazz tempo, set by such black artists as King Oliver, Louis Armstrong, and Duke Ellington and imitated by white musicians. Third, in a generation seeking freedom, the Afro-American symbolized the uninhibited man. Although the image was false, it aroused curiosity about black Americans.

Fourth, and probably most important, were the efforts of black men anxious to inform the nation about the contributions and potential of black Americans. The National Association for the Advancement of Colored People, more than a decade old, formed a platform on which W. E. B. DuBois and James Weldon Johnson, both literary artists, brought Negroes to American attention. Pushing back the curtains of historical research, Carter G. Woodson revealed the black man's role in building the nation. Alain Locke—Ph.D. from Harvard, Rhodes Scholar, aesthetician, philosopher—persuaded young black writers, painters, and dancers to seek their subjects and styles in their African and Afro-American heritage. Charles S. Johnson, editor of *Opportunity* magazine, sought black writers.

These four forces combined to cast a spotlight on Afro-Americans. And a young, confident, educated generation of black writers was prepared to meet the challenge.

Needless to say, short story writers want and need to be published. Outlets appeared during the Twenties. *The Crisis*, official organ of the NAACP, and *Opportunity*, the organ of the National

Urban League, encouraged literary attention through book reviews, literary columns, and annual contests. Little magazines such
as *Fire* and *Palms* came into existence, lasted an issue or two, then
died, but not before they had introduced new writers. And the
more prestigious magazines not only accepted works by Negroes
but, capitalizing on the rage, even requested such materials. For
instance, *Survey Graphic* devoted an entire issue to a presentation
of the culture of the "new" Negro. For three successive years, *The
Carolina*, literary magazine of the University of North Carolina,
reserved a spring issue for literature by Negroes.

The young black writers responded. Two generations removed
from slavery, bolstered by their education, flattered by the attention, they wrote. Jean Toomer lyrically sketched life in Georgia,
Washington, and Chicago. Wallace Thurman satirized Negroes;
Langston Hughes satirized both whites and blacks. Eric Walrond
wrote sultry stories revealing the emotions of Caribbean natives;
Rudolph Fisher depicted the people of Harlem. Zora Neale Hurston told about black people of Florida. John Matheus, Claude
McKay, and Arna Bontemps were among others.

These new writers freed themselves from some psychological
restrictions which had repressed Dunbar and Chesnutt. In many
stories Dunbar had written humorously of stereotyped Southern
darkies; these characters appealed to his editors and publishers.
Even more often, however, he had stressed the virtues of Afro-
Americans—their generosity, their charity, their love, their loyal-
ty, their sense of duty, their honor; his purpose had been to
persuade his white readers that black Americans were worthy to
share the opportunities granted to other Americans. Chesnutt too
had written with a purpose. Contemptuous of the slaves who
remained loyal to their masters, he wrote instead about free mu-
lattoes who equalled or surpassed the intelligence and honor of
their white neighbors.

Young blacks of the Twenties, however, saw less need to "put
forward the best foot of the race." They laughed at and with their
amoral, irresponsible protagonists. Sometimes in the opinion of
older and more conservative critics, such as W. E. B. DuBois and
Benjamin Brawley, they seemed to go too far in reporting publicly
the human frailties which the race had concealed for fear of
further criticism by white America.

The Twenties rocketed young black short story writers into
public prominence, but the Thirties dropped them into the reality
of depression. It is true that they were not neglected as completely
as they had been between 1910 and 1920: *Crisis* and *Opportunity*

continued to publish creative works; Langston Hughes collected his stories into *The Ways of White Folks* (1934); such reputable journals as *The New Republic* and *Esquire* published Ted Poston and Chester Himes among others; new novelists emerged; and helpful assistance came from the Federal Workers Project and new left-wing magazines. The American public was interested in writings by Afro-Americans, but it did not seek them as eagerly as it had during the Twenties.

The pendulum reversed its swing with the advent of Richard Wright, who, in 1938, published *Uncle Tom's Children,* a collection of short stories about people trapped by the violence which Wright believed to be continuously surrounding the Southern black man. Wright wrote obvious propaganda in his stories; some critics have even accused him of being overly melodramatic. Nevertheless, he demonstrated an unmistakable power and artistry which won new respect for the Afro-American writers.

Wright was soon imitated by others. Chester Himes wrote colorful, violent stories about the people of Harlem. Willard Motley and Ann Petry earned praise as short story writers before they concentrated their talents on novels. Frank Yerby wrote protest in the Wright tradition before he too moved on to fame and fortune as a novelist.

In the late Forties and Fifties the list of significant short story writers grew to proportions which cannot be encompassed within a brief introduction. The most prominent are probably Ralph Ellison, James Baldwin, Mary Ellen Vroman ("See How They Run," the story of a school teacher and her pupils), William Melvin Kelley, John Killens, John A. Williams, Julian Mayfield, Ernest Gaines, Kristin Hunter, and Le Roi Jones.

The increase can be attributed to several causes. A first is education. More black Americans than ever before are attending school, where they are probably receiving a better quality of education—as are non-black Americans. From numbers alone, even if the percentage remained constant, one might expect to find more black writers coming from the schools of America. Nevertheless, improved education should not be emphasized to the extreme reflected by scholars who write as though black authors did not exist before World War II or as though black Americans were disinterested in their economic, political, and social conditions before 1950.

There are more important causes. One, the generation of writers after Wright understood that their success depended upon the quality rather than the subject of their work. Instead of hoping to sell a story merely because it was about Negroes, they struggled to develop themselves as artists. An even more important reason is that black men now perceive that the writing of fiction can lead to fame and fortune. As long as chances for success seem impossible in literature or any other activity, talented individuals will concentrate their efforts in more promising areas. But, once the opportunity becomes apparent, many will try. The success of Richard Wright inspired Ellison, Yerby, Motley, and Baldwin. These, in turn, encouraged the present generation. As long as the opportunity continues, talented black Americans will try their hand at stories, and many will succeed.

Charles Waddell Chesnutt
(1858-1932)

Po' Sandy

Charles Waddell Chesnutt was the first Afro-American to master the short story as an art form. Born in Cleveland, Ohio, he was reared in North Carolina, where he became a school teacher at the age of sixteen. After training himself in stenography, he moved North to work briefly as a typist, write fiction, and practice law.

According to popular tradition, Chesnutt's desire to be a writer was inspired by his reading of a novel by Albion Tourgée (*A Fool's Errand*, 1880). Not knowing about William Wells Brown's *Clotel* (1852), Chesnutt decided to be the first Afro-American to write a novel about his race. Although his first story, "The Goophered Grapevine," appeared in *The Atlantic Monthly* in 1887, thirteen years passed before he realized his ambition to publish a novel.

A mulatto, Chesnutt was deeply concerned with the psychological and social problems of Negroes in the North and the South. He examined these problems in *The Wife of His Youth and Other Stories of the Color Line* (1899) and in such novels as *The House Behind the Cedars* (1900), *The Marrow of Tradition* (1901), and *The Colonel's Dream* (1905). His most significant contribution to American literature, however, may be the tales of *The Conjure Woman*, based on folklore which he had heard in North Carolina. The tales are narrated by Uncle Julius, a shrewd ex-slave, who uses them as a means of instructing and manipulating his Northern employer.

From *The Conjure Woman and Other Tales* (Boston: Houghton Mifflin, 1899).

Po' Sandy

On the northeast corner of my vineyard in central North Carolina, and fronting on the Lumberton plank-road, there stood a small frame house, of the simplest construction. It was built of pine lumber, and contained but one room, to which one window gave light and one door admission. Its weather-beaten sides revealed a virgin innocence of paint. Against one end of the house, and occupying half its width, there stood a huge brick chimney: the crumbling mortar had left large cracks between the bricks; the bricks themselves had begun to scale off in large flakes, leaving the chimney sprinkled with unsightly blotches. These evidences of decay were but partially concealed by a creeping vine, which extended its slender branches hither and thither in an ambitious but futile attempt to cover the whole chimney. The wooden shutter, which had once protected the unglazed window, had fallen from its hinges, and lay rotting in the rank grass and jimson-weeds beneath. This building, I learned when I bought the place, had been used as a schoolhouse for several years prior to the breaking out of the war, since which time it had remained unoccupied, save when some stray cow or vagrant hog had sought shelter within its walls from the chill rains and nipping winds of winter.

One day my wife requested me to build her a new kitchen. The house erected by us, when we first came to live upon the vineyard, contained a very conveniently arranged kitchen; but for some occult reason my wife wanted a kitchen in the back yard, apart from the dwelling-house, after the usual Southern fashion. Of course I had to build it.

To save expense, I decided to tear down the old schoolhouse, and use the lumber, which was in a good state of preservation, in the construction of the new kitchen. Before demolishing the old house, however, I made an estimate of the amount of material contained in it, and found that I would have to buy several hundred feet of lumber additional, in order to build the new kitchen according to my wife's plan.

One morning old Julius McAdoo, our colored coachman, harnessed the gray mare to the rockaway, and drove my wife and me over to the sawmill from which I meant to order the new lumber. We drove down the long lane which led from our house to the plank-road; following the plank-road for about a mile, we turned into a road running through the forest and across the swamp to the sawmill beyond. Our carriage jolted over the half-rotten cor-duroy road which traversed the swamp, and then climbed the long hill leading to the sawmill. When he reached the mill, the foreman had gone over to a neighboring farmhouse, probably to smoke or gossip, and we were compelled to await his return before we could transact our business. We remained seated in the carriage, a few rods from the mill, and watched the leisurely movements of the mill-hands. We had not waited long before a huge pine log was placed in position, the machinery of the mill was set in motion, and the circular saw began to eat its way through the log, with a loud whir which resounded throughout the vicinity of the mill. The sound rose and fell in a sort of rhythmic cadence, which, heard from where we sat, was not unpleasing, and not loud enough to prevent conversation. When the saw started on its second journey through the log, Julius observed, in a lugubrious tone, and with a perceptible shudder:—

"Ugh! but dat des do cuddle my blood!"

"What's the matter, Uncle Julius?" inquired my wife, who is of a very sympathetic turn of mind. "Does the noise affect your nerves?"

"No, Mis' Annie," replied the old man, with emotion, "I ain' narvous; but dat saw, a-cuttin' en grindin' thoo dat stick er tim-ber, en moanin', en groanin', en sweekin', kyars my 'memb'ance back ter ole times, en 'min's me er po' Sandy." The pathetic intonation with which he lengthened out the "po' Sandy" touched a responsive chord in our own hearts.

"And who was poor Sandy?" asked my wife, who takes a deep interest in the stories of plantation life which she hears from the lips of the older colored people. Some of these stories are quaintly humorous; others wildly extravagant, revealing the Oriental cast of the negro's imagination; while others, poured freely into the sympathetic ear of a Northern-bred woman, disclose many a tragic incident of the darker side of slavery.

"Sandy," said Julius, in reply to my wife's question, "was a nigger w'at useter b'long ter ole Mars Marrabo McSwayne. Mars Marrabo's place wuz on de yuther side'n de swamp, right nex' ter yo' place. Sandy wuz a monst'us good nigger, en could do so many things erbout a plantation, en alluz 'ten' ter his wuk so well, dat w'en Mars Marrabo's chilluns growed up en married off, dey all un 'em wanted dey daddy fer ter gin 'em Sandy fer a weddin' present. But Mars Marrabo knowed de res' would n' be satisfied ef he gin Sandy ter a'er one un 'em; so w'en day wuz all done married, he fix

it by 'lowin' one er his chilluns ter take Sandy fer a mont' er so, en
den ernudder for a mont' er so, en so on dat erway tel dey had all
had 'im de same lenk er time; en den dey would all take him roun'
ag'in, 'cep'n' oncet in a w'ile w'en Mars Marrabo would len' 'im ter
some er his yuther kinfolks 'roun' de country, w'en dey wuz short
er han's; tel bimeby it got so Sandy did n' hardly knowed whar he
wuz gwine ter stay fum one week's een' ter de yuther.

"One time w'en Sandy wuz lent out ez yushal, a spekilater come
erlong wid a lot er niggers, en Mars Marrabo swap' Sandy's wife
off fer a noo 'oman. W'en Sandy come back, Mars Marrabo gin 'im
a dollar, en 'lowed he wuz monst'us sorry fer ter break up de
fambly, but de spekilater had gin 'im big boot, en times wuz hard
en money skase, en so he wuz bleedst ter make de trade. Sandy tuk
on some 'bout losin' his wife, but he soon seed dey want no use
cryin' ober spilt merlasses; en bein' ez he lacked de looks er de noo
'oman, he tuk up wid her atter she'd be'n on de plantation a mont'
er so.

"Sandy en his noo wife got on mighty well tergedder, en de
niggers all 'mence' ter talk about how lovin' dey wuz. W'en Tenie
wuz tuk sick oncet, Sandy useter set up all night wid 'er, en den go
ter wuk in de mawnin' des lack he had his reg'lar sleep; en Tenie
would 'a' done anythin' in de worl' for her Sandy.

"Sandy en Tenie had n' be'n libbin' tergedder fer mo' d'n two
mont's befo' Mars Marrabo's old uncle, w'at libbed down in Robeson County, sent up ter fin' out ef Mars Marrabo could n' len' 'im
er hire 'im a good han' fer a mont' er so. Sandy's marster wuz one
er dese yer easy-gwine folks w'at wanter please eve'ybody, en he
says yas, he could len' 'im Sandy. En Mars Marrabo tol' Sandy fer
ter git ready ter go down ter Robeson nex' day, fer ter stay a mont'
er so.

"It wuz monst'us hard on Sandy fer ter take 'im 'way fum .
Tenie. It wuz so fur down ter Robeson dat he did n' hab no chance
er comin' back ter see her tel de time wuz up; he would n' 'a' mine
comin' ten er fifteen mile at night ter see Tenie, but Mars Marrabo's uncle's plantation wuz mo' d'n forty mile off. Sandy wuz
mighty sad en cas' down atter w'at Mars Marrabo tol' 'im en he
says ter Tenie, sezee:—

" 'I'm gittin' monst'us ti'ed er dish yer gwine roun' so much.
Here I is lent ter Mars Jeems dis mont', en I got ter do so-en-so;
en ter Mars Archie de nex' mont', en I got ter do so-en-so; den I
got ter go ter Miss Jinnie's: en hit's Sandy dis en Sandy dat, en
Sandy yer en Sandy dere, tel it 'pears ter me I ain' got no home,
ner no marster, ner no mistiss, ner no nuffin. I can't eben keep a

wife: my yuther ole 'oman wuz sol' away widout my gittin' a chance fer ter tell her good-by; en now I got ter go off en leab you, Tenie, en I dunno whe'r I'm eber gwine ter see you ag'in er no. I wisht I wuz a tree, er a stump, er a rock, er sump'n w'at could stay on de plantation fer a w'ile.'

"Atter Sandy got thoo talkin', Tenie did n' say naer word, but des sit dere by de fier, studyin' en studyin'. Bimeby she up'n' says:—

" 'Sandy, is I eber tol' you I wuz a cunjuh 'omen?'

"Co'se Sandy had'n nebber dremp' er nuffin lack dat, en he made a great 'miration w'en he hear w'at Tenie say. Bimeby Tenie went on:—

" 'I ain' goophered nobody, ner done no cunjuh wuk, fer fifteen year er mo'; en w'en I got religion I made up my mine I would n' wuk no mo' goopher. But dey is some things I doan b'lieve it's no sin fer ter do; en ef you doan wanter be sent roun' fum pillar ter pos', en ef you doan wanter go down ter Robeson, I kin fix things so you won't haf ter. Ef you'll des say de word, I kin turn you ter w'ateber you wanter be, en you kin stay right whar you wanter, ez long ez you mineter.'

"Sandy say he doan keer: he's willin' fer ter do anythin' fer ter stay close ter Tenie. Den Tenie ax 'im ef he doan wanter be turnt inter a rabbit.

"Sandy say, 'No, de dogs mought git atter me.'

" 'Shill I turn you ter a wolf?' sez Tenie.

" 'No, eve'ybody's skeered er a wolf, en I doan want nobody ter be skeered er me.'

" 'Shill I turn you ter a mawkin'bird?'

" 'No, a hawk mought ketch me. I wanter be turnt inter sump'n w'at'll stay in one place.'

" 'I kin turn you ter a tree', sez Tenie. 'You won't hab no mouf ner years, but I kin turn you back oncet in a w'ile, so you kin git sump'n ter eat, en hear w'at's gwine on.'

"Well, Sandy say dat'll do. En so Tenie tuk 'im down by de aidge er de swamp, not fur fum de quarters, en turnt 'im inter a big pine-tree, en sot 'im out 'mongs' some yuther trees. En de nex' mawnin', ez some er de fiel' han's wuz gwine long dere, dey seed a tree w'at dey did'n 'member er habbin' seed befo'; it wuz monst'us quare, en dey wuz bleedst ter 'low dat dey had n' 'membered right er e'se one er de saplin's had be'n growin' monst'us fas'.

"W'en Mars Marrabo 'skiver' dat Sandy wuz gone, he 'lowed Sandy had runned away. He got de dogs out, but de las' place dey could track Sandy ter wuz de foot er dat pine-tree. En dere de dogs stood en barked, en bayed, en pawed at de tree, en tried ter climb up on it; en w'en dey wuz tuk roun' thoo de swamp ter look fer de scent, dey broke loose en made fer dat tree ag'in. It wuz de beatenis' thing de w'ite folks eber hearn of, en Mars Marrabo 'lowed dat Sandy must 'a' clim' up on de tree en jump' off on a mule er sump'n, en rid fur ernuff fer ter spile de scent. Mars Marrabo wanted ter 'cuse some er de yuther niggers er heppin' Sandy off, but dey all 'nied it ter de las'; en eve'ybody knowed Tenie sot too much sto' by Sandy fer ter he'p 'im run away whar she could n' nebber see 'im no mo'.

"W'en Sandy had be'n gone long ernuff fer folks ter think he done got clean away, Tenie useter go down ter de woods at night en turn 'im back, en den dey'd slip up ter de cabin en set by de fire en talk. But dey ha' ter be monst'us keerful, er e'se somebody would 'a' seed 'em, en dat would 'a' spile' de whole thing; so Tenie alluz turnt Sandy back in de mawnin' early, befo' anybody wuz a-stirrin'.

"But Sandy did n' git erlong widout his trials en tribberlations. One day a woodpecker come erlong en 'mence' ter peck at de tree; en de nex' time Sandy wuz turnt back he had a little roun' hole in his arm, des lack a sharp stick be'n stuck in it. Atter dat Tenie sot a sparrer-hawk fer ter watch de tree; en w'en de woodpecker come erlong nex' mawnin' fer ter finish his nes', he got gobble' up mos' 'fo' he stuck his bill in de bark.

"Nudder time, Mars Marrabo sent a nigger out in de woods fer ter chop tuppentime boxes. De man chop a box in dish yer tree, en hack' de bark up two er th'ee feet, fer ter let de tuppentime run. De nex' time Sandy wuz turnt back he had a big skyar on his lef' leg, des lack it be'n skunt; en it tuk Tenie nigh 'bout all night fer ter fix a mixtry ter kyo it up. Atter dat, Tenie sot a hawnet fer ter watch de tree; en w'en de nigger come back ag'in fer ter cut ernudder box on de yuther side'n de tree, de hawnet stung 'im so hard dat de ax slip en cut his foot nigh 'bout off.

"W'en Tenie see so many things happenin' ter de tree, she 'cluded she'd ha' ter turn Sandy ter sump'n e'se; en atter studyin' de matter ober, en talkin' wid Sandy one ebenin', she made up her mine fer ter fix up a goopher mixtry w'at would turn herse'f en Sandy ter foxes, er sump'n, so dey could run away en go some'rs whar dey could be free en lib lack w'ite folks.

"But dey ain' no tellin' w'at's gwine ter happen in dis worl'. Tenie had got de night sot fer her en Sandy ter run away, w'en dat ve'y day one er Mars Marrabo's sons rid up ter de big house in his buggy, en say his wife wuz monst'us sick, en he want his mammy ter len' 'im a 'oman fer ter nuss his wife. Tenie's mistiss say sen' Tenie; she wuz a good nuss. Young mars wuz in a tarrible hurry fer ter git back home. Tenie wuz washin' at de big house dat day, en her mistiss say she should go right 'long wid her young marster. Tenie tried ter make some 'scuse fer ter git away en hide 'tel night, we'n she would have eve'ything fix' up fer her en Sandy; she say she wanter go ter her cabin fer ter git her bonnet. Her mistiss say it doan matter 'bout de bonnet; her head-hankcher wuz good ernuff. Den Tenie say she wanter git her bes' frock; her mistiss say no, she doan need no mo' frock, en w'en dat one got dirty she could git a clean one whar she wuz gwine. So Tenie had ter git in de buggy en go 'long wid young Mars Dunkin ter his plantation, w'ich wuz mo' d'n twenty mile away; en dey wa'n't no chance er her seein' Sandy no mo' 'tel she come back home. De po' gal felt monst'us bad 'bout de way things wuz gwine on, en she knowed Sandy mus' be a wond'rin' why she did n' come en turn 'im back no mo'.

"W'iles Tenie wuz away nussin' young Mars Dunkin's wife, Mars Marrabo tuk a notion fer ter buil' 'im a noo kitchen; en bein' ez he had lots er timber on his place, he begun ter look 'roun' fer a tree ter hab de lumber sawed out'n. En I dunno how it come to be so, but he happen fer ter hit on de ve'y tree w'at Sandy wuz turnt inter. Tenie wuz gone, en dey wa'n't nobody ner nuffin fer ter watch de tree.

"De two men w'at cut de tree down say dey nebber had sech a time wid a tree befo': dey axes would glansh off, en did n' 'pear ter make no prōgress thoo de wood; en of all de creakin', en shakin', en wobblin' you eber see, dat tree done it w'en it commence' ter fall. It wuz de beatenis' thing!

"W'en dey got de tree all trim' up, dey chain it up ter a timber waggin, en start fer de sawmill. But dey had a hard time gittin' de log dere: fus' dey got stuck in de mud w'en day wuz gwine crosst de swamp, en it wuz two er th'ee hours befo' dey could git out. W'en dey start' on ag'in, de chain kep' a-comin' loose, en dey had ter keep a-stoppin' en a-stoppin' fer ter hitch de log up ag'in. W'en dey commence' ter climb de hill ter de sawmill, de log broke loose, en roll down de hill en in 'mongs' de trees, en hit tuk nigh 'bout half a day mo' ter git it haul' up ter de sawmill.

"De nex' mawnin' atter de day de tree wuz haul' ter de sawmill, Tenie come home. W'en she got back ter her cabin, de fus' thing she done wuz ter run down ter de woods en see how Sandy wuz

gittin' on. W'en she seed de stump standin' dere, wid de sap
runnin' out'n it, en de limbs layin' scattered roun', she night 'bout
went out'n her min'. She run ter her cabin, en got her goopher
mixtry, en den follered de track er de timber waggin ter de sawmill. She knowed Sandy could n' lib mo' d'n a minute er so ef she
turnt him back, fer he wuz all chop' up so he 'd 'a' be'n bleedst ter
die. But she wanted ter turn 'im back long ernuff fer ter 'splain ter
'im dat she had n' went off a-purpose, en lef' 'im ter be chop' down
en sawed up. She did n' want Sandy ter die wid no hard feelin's
to'ds her.

"De han's at de sawmill had des got de big log on de kerridge,
en wuz startin' up de saw, w'en dey seed a 'oman runnin' up de
hill, all out er bref, cryin' en gwine on des lack she wuz plumb
'stracted. It wuz Tenie; she come right inter de mill, en th'owed
herse'f on de log, right in front er de saw, a-hollerin' en cryin' ter
her Sandy ter fergib her, en not ter think hard er her, fer it wa'n't
no fault er hern. Den Tenie 'membered de tree did n' hab no years,
en she wuz gittin' ready fer ter wuk her goopher mixtry so ez ter
turn Sandy back, w'en de mill-hands kotch holt er her en tied her
arms wid a rope, en fasten' her to one er de posts in de sawmill; en
den dey started de saw up ag'in, en cut de log up inter bo'ds en
scantlin's right befo' her eyes. But it wuz mighty hard wuk; fer of
all de sweekin', en moanin', en groanin', dat log done it w'iles de
saw wuz a-cuttin' thoo it. De saw wuz one er dese yer old-timey,
up-en-down saws, en hit tuk longer dem days ter saw a log 'en it
do now. Dey greased de saw, but dat did n' stop de fuss; hit kep'
right on, tel fin'ly dey got de log all sawed up.

"W'en de oberseah w'at run de sawmill come fum breakfas', de
han's up en tell him 'bout de crazy 'oman—ez dey s'posed she
wuz—w'at had come runnin' in de sawmill, a-hollerin' en gwine
on, en tried ter th'ow herse'f befo' de saw. En de oberseah sent two
er th'ee er de han's fer ter take Tenie back ter her marster's
plantation.

"Tenie 'peared ter be out'n her min' fer a long time, en her
marster ha' ter lock her up in de smoke-'ouse 'tel she got ober her
spells. Mars Marrabo wuz monst'us mad, en hit would 'a' made yo'
flesh crawl fer ter hear him cuss, 'caze he say de spekilater w'at he
got Tenie fum had fooled 'im by wukkin' a crazy 'oman off on
him. W'iles Tenie wuz lock up in de smoke-'ouse, Mars Marrabo
tuk 'n' haul de lumber fum de sawmill, en put up his noo kitchen.

"W'en Tenie got quiet' down, so she could be 'lowed ter go 'round' de plantation, she up'n' tole her marster all erbout Sandy cn de pine-tree; en w'en Mars Marrabo hearn it, he 'lowed she wuz de wuss 'stracted nigger he eber hearn of. He did n' know w'at ter do wid Tenie: fus' he thought he'd put her in de po'-house; but fin'ly, seein' ez she did n' do no harm ter nobody ner nuffin, but des went 'roun' moanin', en groanin', en shakin' her head, he 'cluded ter let her stay on de plantation en nuss de little nigger chilluns w'en dey mammies wuz ter wuk in de cotton-fiel'.

"De noo kitchen Mars Marrabo buil' wuz n' much use, fer it had n' be'n put up long befo' de niggers 'mence' ter notice quare things erbout it. Dey could hear sump'n moanin' en groanin' 'bout de kitchen in de night-time, en w'en de win' would blow dey could hear sump'n a-hollerin' en sweekin' lack it wuz in great pain en sufferin'. En it got so atter a w'ile dat it wuz all Mars Marrabo's wife could do ter git a 'oman ter stay in de kitchen in de daytime long ernuff ter do de cookin'; en dey wa'n't naer nigger on de plantation w'at would n' rudder take forty dan ter go 'bout dat kitchen atter dark,—dat is, 'cep'n' Tenie; she did n' 'pear ter min' de ha'nts. She useter slip 'roun' at night, en set on de kitchen steps, en lean up agin de do'-jamb, en run on ter herse'f wid some kine er foolishness w'at nobody could n' make out; fer Mars Marrabo had th'eaten' ter sen' her off'n de plantation ef she say anything ter any er de yuther niggers 'bout de pine-tree. But somehow er 'nudder de niggers foun' out all erbout it, en dey all knowed de kitchen wuz ha'nted by Sandy's sperrit. En bimeby hit got so Mars Marrabo's wife herse'f wuz skeered ter go out in de yard atter dark.

"W'en it come ter dat, Mars Marrabo tuk en to' de kitchen down, en use' de lumber fer ter buil' dat ole school'ouse w'at you er talkin' 'bout pullin' down. De school'ouse wuz n' use' 'cep'n' in de daytime, en on dark nights folks gwine 'long de road would hear quare soun's en see quare things. Po' ole Tenie useter go down dere at night, en wander 'roun' de school'ouse; en de niggers all 'lowed she went fer ter talk wid Sandy's sperrit. En one winter mawnin', w'en one er de boys went ter school early fer ter start de fire, w'at should he fin' but po' ole Tenie, layin' on de flo', stiff en col', en dead. Dere did n' 'pear ter be nuffin pertickler de matter wid her,—she had des grieve' herse'f ter def fer her Sandy. Mars Marrabo did n' shed no tears. He thought Tenie wuz crazy, en dey wa'n't no tellin' w'at she mought do nex'; en dey ain' much room in dis worl' fer crazy w'ite folks, let 'lone a crazy nigger.

"Hit wa'n't long atter dat befo' Mars Marrabo sol' a piece er his track er lan' ter Mars Dugal' McAdoo,—*my* old marster,—en dat's how de ole school'ouse happen to be on yo' place. W'en de wah broke out, de school stop', en de ole school'ouse be'n stannin' empty ever sence,—dat is, 'cep'n' fer de ha'nts. En folks sez dat de ole school'ouse, er any yuther house w'at got any er dat lumber in it w'at wuz sawed out'n de tree w'at Sandy wuz turnt inter, is gwine ter be ha'nted tel de las' piece er plank is rotted en crumble' inter dus'."

Annie had listened to this gruesome narrative with strained attention.

"What a system it was," she exclaimed, when Julius had finished, "under which such things were possible!"

"What things?" I asked, in amazement. "Are you seriously considering the possibility of a man's being turned into a tree?"

"Oh, no," she replied quickly, "not that;" and then she murmured absently, and with a dim look in her fine eyes, "Poor Tenie!"

We ordered the lumber, and returned home. That night, after we had gone to bed, and my wife had to all appearances been sound asleep for half an hour, she startled me out of an incipient doze by exclaiming suddenly,—

"John, I don't believe I want my new kitchen built out of the lumber in that old schoolhouse."

"You wouldn't for a moment allow yourself," I replied, with some asperity, "to be influenced by that absurdly impossible yarn which Julius was spinning to-day?"

"I know the story is absurd," she replied dreamily, "and I am not so silly as to believe it. But I don't think I should ever be able to take any pleasure in that kitchen if it were built out of that lumber. Besides, I think the kitchen would look better and last longer if the lumber were all new."

Of course she had her way. I bought the new lumber, though not without grumbling. A week or two later I was called away from home on business. On my return, after an absence of several days, my wife remarked to me,—

"John, there has been a split in the Sandy Run Colored Baptist Church, on the temperance question. About half the members have come out from the main body, and set up for themselves. Uncle Julius is one of the seceders, and he came to me yesterday and asked if they might not hold their meetings in the old schoolhouse for the present."

"I hope you didn't let the old rascal have it," I returned, with some warmth. I had just received a bill for the new lumber I had bought.

"Well," she replied, "I couldn't refuse him the use of the house for so good a purpose."

"And I'll venture to say," I continued, "that you subscribed something toward the support of the new church?"

She did not attempt to deny it.

"What are they going to do about the ghost?" I asked, somewhat curious to know how Julius would get around this obstacle.

"Oh," replied Annie, "Uncle Julius says that ghosts never disturb religious worship, but that if Sandy's spirit *should* happen to stray into meeting by mistake, no doubt the preaching would do it good."

Paul Laurence Dunbar
(1872-1906)

The Mortification of the Flesh *and* Mr. Cornelius Johnson, Office-Seeker

The son of former slaves, Paul Laurence Dunbar, born in Dayton, Ohio, was the best known and most popular Afro-American writer of his generation. While working as an elevator operator (the best job he could find as a black man with a high school education), he published two books of poetry—*Oak and Ivy* (1892) and *Majors and Minors* (1896). The second impressed William Dean Howells, who enthusiastically praised him as "the first American Negro to evince innate artistic talent." The success of *Lyrics of Lowly Life* (1896) prompted Dunbar to concentrate on a career as a writer and public reader. Despite failing health, which caused an early death, he published three additional volumes of poetry, four novels, four collections of stories, lyrics for musical shows, and numerous articles and stories which have not been collected.

Dunbar's literary reputation is based upon his poetry, which is superior to his fiction. Nevertheless, his stories often reveal the perceptive characterization and the light satire which constitute a major part of his talent as a writer. In fiction Dunbar is best known for stories about life on the plantations either before or shortly after the Civil War. The following stories, however, reveal Dunbar's interest in other themes too frequently ignored by his critics.

"The Mortification of the Flesh" from *Lippincott's Magazine,* LXVII (September, 1901).

"Mr. Cornelius Johnson, Office-seeker" from *The Strength of Gideon and Other Stories* (New York: Dodd, Mead, 1900).

"The Mortification of the Flesh" is one of a series of "Ohio Pastorals," which Dunbar wrote for *Lippincott's Magazine*. The characters in the stories are white.

The Mortification of the Flesh

First in a Series of Ohio Pastorals

Nathan Foster and his life-long friend and neighbor, Silas Bollender, sat together side by side upon the line fence that separated their respective domains. They were both whittling away industriously, and there had been a long silence between them. Nathan broke it, saying, " 'Pears to me like I've had oncommon good luck this year."

Silas paused and carefully scrutinized the stick he was whittling into nothing at all, and then resumed operations on it before he returned: "Well, you have had good luck, there ain't no denyin' that. It 'pears as though you've been ee-specially blest."

"An' I know I ain't done nothin' to deserve it."

"No, of course not. Don't take no credit to yoreself, Nathan. We don't none of us deserve our blessin's, however we may feel about our crosses: we kin be purty shore o' that."

"Now look," Nathan went on; "my pertater vines was like little trees, an' nary a bug on 'em."

"An' you had as good a crop o' corn as I've ever seen raised in this part o' Montgomery County."

"Yes, an' I sold it, too, jest before that big drop in the price."

"After givin' away all the turnips you could, you had to feed 'em to the hogs."

"My fruit-trees jest had to be propped up, an' I've got enough perserves in my cellar to last two er three winters, even takin' into consideration the drain o' church socials an' o' cherity."

"Yore chickens air fat an' sassy, not a sign o' pip among 'em."

"Look at them cows in the fur pasture. Did you ever seen anything to beat 'em fur sleekness?"

"Well, look at the pasture itself: it's most enough to make human bein's envy the critters. You didn't have a drop o' rain on you while you was gettin' yore hay in, did you?"

"Not a drop."

"An' I had a whole lot ruined jest as I was about to rick it."

So, alternately, they went on enumerating Nathan's blessings, until it seemed that there was nothing left for him to desire.

"Silas," he said solemnly, "sich luck as I'm a-havin' is achilly skerry; it don't seem right."

Silas had a droll humor of his own, and his eyes twinkled as he said: "No, it don't seem right fur a religious man like you, Nathan. Ef you was a hard an' graspin' sinner it 'u'd be jest what a body'd 'spect. You could understand it then: the Lord 'u'd jest be makin' you topheavy so's yore fall 'u'd be the greater."

"I do' know but what that's it anyhow. Mebbe I'm a-gittin' puffed up over my goods without exactly knowin' it."

"Mebbe so, mebbe so. Them kind o' feelin's is mighty sneaky comin' on a body. O' course, I ain't seen no signs of it yit in you; but it 'pears to me you'll have to mortify yore flesh yit to keep from bein' purse-proud."

"Mortify the flesh," repeated Nathan seriously.

"O' course, you can't put peas in yore shoes er git any of yore friends to lash you, so you'll have to find some other way o' mortifyin' yore flesh. Well, fur my part, I don't need to look fur none, fur I never had too many blessin's in my life, less'n you'd want to put the children under that head."

Silas shut up his jack-knife with a snap and, laughing, slid down on his side of the fence. In serious silence Nathan Foster watched him go stumping up the path towards his house. "Silas seems to take everything so light in this world," he breathed half aloud. "I wonder how he can do it."

With Nathan, now, it was just the other way. Throughout his eight-and-forty years he had taken every fact of life with ponderous seriousness. Entirely devoid of humor, he was a firm believer in signs, omens, tokens, and judgments. Though the two men had grown up together and been friends from a boyhood spent upon their fathers' adjoining farms, their lives had been two very different stories. Silas, looking on everything cheerily, had married early and was the father of a houseful of children. His wife ruled him with a rod of iron, but he accepted her domination quite as a matter of course and went merrily on his way. He had never been a very successful man, but he had managed to hold the old homestead and feed and clothe his family. This seemed entirely to satisfy him.

On the other hand, to Nathan marriage had always seemed an undertaking fraught with so much danger that he had feared to embark upon it, and although in his younger days his heart had

often burned within him when he contemplated some charming
damsel, these heart-burnings had gone unknown to anyone but
himself until someone else had led the girl to the altar. So he was
set down as not a marrying man. He was essentially a cautious
man, and through caution and industry his means had grown until
from being well-to-do the people of Montgomery County spoke of
him as a rich old bachelor. He was a religious man, and with the
vision of Dives in his mind his wealth oppressed and frightened him.
He gave to his church and gave freely. But he had the instinct for
charity without the faculty for it. And he was often held back
from good deeds by a modesty which told him that his gifts would
be looked upon as "Alms to be seen of men."

As usual, he had taken his friend's bantering words in hard
earnest and was turning them over in his mind. When the bell
rang, calling him in to supper, he flung the stick which he had been
whittling into the middle of the potato patch and stood watching
abstractedly where it fell. Then, as if talking to it, he murmured,
"Mortification of the flesh," and started moving slowly to the
kitchen.

The next morning, when Nathan and Silas met to compare
notes, the former began, "I been thinking over what you said last
night, Silas, about me mortifying my flesh, and it seems to me like
a good idee."

Silas looked at him quizzically from beneath bent brows, but
Nathan went on, "I wrasseled in prayer last night, and it was
shown to me that it wa'n't no more'n right fur me to make some
kind o' sacrifice fur the mercies that's been bestowed upon me."

"Well, I do' know, Nathan; burnt offerings air a little out now."

"I don't mean nothin' like that; I mean some sacrifice of myself;
some——"

His sentence was broken in upon by a shrill voice that called
from Silas Bollender's kitchen door: "Si, you'd better be gittin'
about yore work instid o' standin' over there a-gassin' all the
mornin'. I'm shore I don't have no time to stand around."

"All right, Mollie," he called back to his wife, and then, turning
to Nathan, he said, "Speakin' of mortifyin' the flesh an' makin' a
sacrifice of yoreself, why don't you git married?"

Nathan started.

"Then, you see," Silas continued, "you'd be shore to accomplish
both. Fur pure mortification of the flesh, I don't know of nothin'
more thorough-goin' er effectiver than a wife. Also she is a vex-

ation of the sperrit. Look at me an' Mis' Bollender, fur instance.
Do you think I need a hair shirt when I think I'm gittin' over-fed?
No. Mis' Bollender keeps me with a meek an' subdued sperrit. You
raaly ought to marry, Nathan."

"Do you think so?"

"It looks like to me that that 'u'd be about as good a sacrifice as
you could make, an' then it's sich a lastin' one."

"I don't believe that you realize what you air a-sayin', Silas. It's
a mighty desprit step that you're advisin' me to take."

Again Mrs. Bollender's voice broke in, "Si, air you goin' to git
anything done this mornin', er air you goin' to stand there an' hold
up that fence fur the rest o' the day?"

"Nathan," said Silas, "kin you stand here an' listen to a voice
an' a speech like that an' then ask me ef I realize the despritness
of marriage?"

"It's desprit," said Nathan pensively, "but who'd you advise me
to marry, Silas, ef I did,—that is, ef I did make up my mind to
marry,—an' I don' jest see any other way."

"Oh, I ain't pickin' out wives fur anybody, but it seems to me
that you might be doin' a good turn by marryin' the Widder
Young. The Lord 'u'd have two special reasons fur blessin' you
then; fur you'd be mortifyin' yore flesh an' at the same time
a-helpin' the widder an' orphans."

Nathan turned his honest gray eyes upon his friend, but there
was a guilty flush upon his sunburned cheek as he said, "That's
so." For the world, he couldn't admit to Silas that he had been
thinking hard of the Widow Young even before he had thought of
mortifying his flesh with a wife. Now that he had an added excuse
for keeping her in his mind, he was guiltily conscious of trying to
cheat himself,—of passing off a pleasure for a penance. But his
wavering determination was strengthened by the reflection that it
was about Mrs. Young, not as a widow, but as a wife and a means
of grace, that he was concerned, and the memory of what Silas had
said about wives in general had put him right with his conscience
again.

The widow was a lively, buxom woman who had seen forty busy
summers pass. She had been one of the prettiest and most industri-
ous girls of the village, and it had seemed that Nathan, when a
young man, had serious intentions towards her. But his extreme
caution had got the better of his inclination, and she had been
retired to that limbo where he kept all his secret heart-burnings.

She had married a ne'er-do-weel, and until the day of his death, leaving her with two children on her hands, she had had need of all her thrift.

Nathan thought of all these things and a lively satisfaction grew up in his mind. He thought of the good his money would do the struggling woman, of the brightness it would bring into her life. "Well, it's good," he murmured; "I'll be killin' two birds with one stone."

Once decided, it did not take him long to put his plans into execution. But he called Silas over to the fence that evening after he had dressed to pay a visit to the widow.

"Well, Silas," he began, "I've determined to take the step you advised."

"Humph, you made up yore mind quick, Nathan."

Nathan blushed, but said, "I do' know as it's any use a-waitin'; ef a thing's to be done, it ought to be done an' got through with."

"I'll have to ask you, now, ef you realize what a desprit step you're a-takin'?"

"I've thought it over prayerfully."

"I don't want nothin' that I said in lightness of mind to influence you. I do' know as I take sich things as serious as I ought."

"Well, I own up you did start the idee in my head, but I've thought it all over sence an' made up my mind fur myself, an' I ain't to be turned now. What I want partic'lar to know now is, whether it wouldn't be best to tell Lizzie—I mean the widder—that I want her as a means of mortification."

"Well, no, Nathan, I do' know as I would do that jest yit; I don't believe it 'u'd be best."

"But ef she don't know, wouldn't it be obtainin' her under false pertenses ef she said yes?"

"Not exactly the way I look at it, fur you've got more motives fur marryin' than one."

"What! Explain yoreself, Silas, explain yoreself."

"I mean you want to do her good as well as subdue yore own sperrit."

"Oh, yes, that's so."

"Now, no woman wants to know at first that she's a vexation to a man's sperrit. It sounds scriptural, but it don't sound nooptial. Now look at me an' Mis' Bollender. I never told her untell we'd been married more'n six months. Fact is, it never occurred to me before. But she didn't believe it then, an' she won't believe it tell this day. She admits that she's my salvation, but not in that way."

Silas chuckled and his friend chewed a straw and thought long. Finally he said: "Well, I'll agree not to tell her right away, but ef she consents, I must tell her a week er so after we're married. It'll ease my conscience. If I could tell her now, it 'ud be a heap easier in gittin' 'round to the question. I don't know jest how to do it without."

"Oh, you won't have no trouble in makin' her understand. Matrimony's a subjic' that women air mighty keen on. They can see that a man's poppin' the question ef he only half tries. You'll git through all right."

Somewhat strengthened, Nathan left his friend and sought the widow's house. He found her stitching merrily away under the light of a coal-oil lamp with a red shade. Even in his trepidation he found secret satisfaction in the red glow that filled the room and glorified the widow's brown hair.

"La, Nathan," said the widow when he was seated, "who'd 'a' expected to see you up here? You've got to be sich a home body that no one don't look to see you outside o' yore own field an' garden."

"I jest thought I'd drop in," said Nathan.

"Well, it's precious kind o' you, I'm shore. I was a-feelin' kind o' lonesome. The children go to bed with the chickens."

For an instant there was a picture in his mind of just such another evening as this, with the children all in bed and the widow sitting across from him or even beside him in another room than this. His heart throbbed, but the picture vanished before his realization of the stern necessity of saying something.

"I jest thought I'd drop in," he said. Then his face reddened as he remembered that he had said that before. But the widow was fully equal to the occasion.

"Well, it does remind me of old times to see you jest droppin' in informal-like, this way. My, how time does fly!"

"It is like old times, ain't it?"

Here they found a common subject, and the talk went on more easily, aided by story and reminiscence. When Nathan began to take account of the time, he found with alarm that two hours had passed without his getting any nearer to his object. From then he attempted to talk of one thing while thinking of another and failed signally. The conversation wavered, recovered itself, wavered again, and then it fell flat.

Nathan saw that his time had come. He sighed, cleared his throat, and began: "Widder, I been thinkin' a good deal lately, an'

I been talkin' some with a friend o' mine." He felt guiltily conscious of what that friend had counselled him to keep back. "I've
been greatly prospered in my day; in fact, 'my cup runneth over.' "

"You have been prospered, Nathan."

"Seems's ef—seems's ef I'd ought to sheer it with somebody,
don't it?"

"Well, Nathan, I do' know nobody that's more generous in
givin' to the pore than you air."

"I don't mean jest exactly that way: I mean—widder, you're
the morti—I mean the salvation of my soul. Could you—would
you—er—do you think you'd keer to sheer my blessin's with
me—an' add another one to 'em?"

The Widow Young looked at him in astonishment; then, as she
perceived his drift, the tears filled her eyes and she asked, "Do you
mean it, Nathan?"

"I wouldn't 'a' spent so much labor on a joke, widder."

"No, it don't seem like you would, Nathan. Well, it's sudden,
mighty sudden, but I can't say no."

"Fur these an' all other blessin's make us truly thankful, oh
Lord, we ask fur His name's sake—Amen!" said Nathan devoutly.
And he sat another hour with the widow, making plans for the
early marriage, on which he insisted.

The marriage took place very soon after the brief wooing was
done. But the widow had been settled in Nathan's home over a
month before he had even thought of telling her of the real motive
of his marriage, and every day from the time it occurred to him it
grew harder for him to do.

The charm and comfort of married life had wrapped him about
as with a mantle, and he was at peace with the world. From this
state his conscience pricked him awake, and on a night when he
had been particularly troubled he sought his friend and counsellor
with a clouded brow. They sat together in their accustomed place
on the fence.

"I'm bothered, Silas," said Nathan.

"What's the matter?"

"Why, there's several things. First off, I ain't never told the
widder that she was a mortification, an' next, she ain't. I look
around at that old house o' mine that ain't been a home sence
mother used to scour the hearth an' it makes me feel like singing
fur joy. An' I hear them children playin' round me—they're the
beatenest children; that youngest one called me daddy yistiddy—
well, I see them playin' around an' my eyes air opened, an' I see

that the widder's jest another blessin' added to the rest. It looks to me like I had tried to cheat the Almighty."

With a furtive glance in the direction of his house, Silas took out his pipe and filled it, then between whiffs he said: "Well, now, Nathan, I do' know as you've got any cause to feel bothered. You've done yore duty. Ef you've tried to mortify yore flesh an' it refused to mortify, why, that's all you could do, an' I believe the Lord'll take the will fur the deed an' credit you accordin'ly."

"Mebbe so, Silas, mebbe so; but I've got to do more o' my duty, I've got to tell her."

He slipped down from the fence.

"Nathan," called his crony, but Nathan hurried away as if afraid to trust time with his will. "That's jest like him," said Silas, "to go an' spoil it all;" and he walked down his field-path grumbling to himself.

When the new husband reached the house his courage almost failed him, but he rushed in exclaiming, "Widder, I've got to tell you, you're a mortification of the flesh an' a vexation to the sperrit; long may you continuer fur the good of my soul."

Then, his duty being done and his conscience quieted, he kissed her and took one of the children on his knee.

Critics often accuse Dunbar of refusing to protest publicly against unjust treatment of Negroes. Actually, he could not write realistically about conditions of black Americans in the South because he was unfamiliar with that region. Dunbar, however, understood and described the economic and political problems of black men in the North. "Mr. Cornelius Johnson" is one of several stories in which Dunbar castigated the Republican party for victimizing Negroes.

Mr. Cornelius Johnson, Office-Seeker

It was a beautiful day in balmy May and the sun shone pleasantly on Mr. Cornelius Johnson's very spruce Prince Albert suit of grey as he alighted from the train in Washington. He cast his eyes about him, and then gave a sigh of relief and satisfaction as he

took his bag from the porter and started for the gate. As he went
along, he looked with splendid complacency upon the less fortu-
nate mortals who were streaming out of the day coaches. It was a
Pullman sleeper on which he had come in. Out on the pavement he
hailed a cab, and giving the driver the address of a hotel, stepped
in and was rolled away. Be it said that he had cautiously inquired
about the hotel first and found that he could be accommodated
there.

As he leaned back in the vehicle and allowed his eyes to roam
over the streets, there was an air of distinct prosperity about
him. It was in evidence from the tips of his ample patent-leather
shoes to the crown of the soft felt hat that sat rakishly upon his
head. His entrance into Washington had been long premeditated,
and he had got himself up accordingly.

It was not such an imposing structure as he had fondly imagined, before which the cab stopped and set Mr. Johnson down. But
then he reflected that it was about the only house where he could
find accommodation at all, and he was content. In Alabama one
learns to be philosophical. It is good to be philosophical in a place
where the proprietor of a café fumbles vaguely around in the
region of his hip pocket and insinuates that he doesn't want one's
custom. But the visitor's ardor was not cooled for all that. He
signed the register with a flourish, and bestowed a liberal fee upon
the shabby boy who carried his bag to his room.

"Look here, boy," he said, "I am expecting some callers soon. If
they come, just send them right up to my room. You take good
care of me and look sharp when I ring and you'll not lose anything."

Mr. Cornelius Johnson always spoke in a large and important
tone. He said the simplest thing with an air so impressive as to
give it the character of a pronouncement. Indeed, his voice naturally was round, mellifluous and persuasive. He carried himself
always as if he were passing under his own triumphal arch. Perhaps, more than anything else, it was these qualities of speech and
bearing that had made him invaluable on the stump in the recent
campaign in Alabama. Whatever it was that held the secret of his
power, the man and principles for which he had labored
triumphed, and he had come to Washington to reap his reward. He
had been assured that his services would not be forgotten, and it
was no intention of his that they should be.

After a while he left his room and went out, returning later with
several gentlemen from the South and a Washington man. There is

some freemasonry among these office-seekers in Washington that throws them inevitably together. The men with whom he returned were such characters as the press would designate as "old wheel-horses" or "pillars of the party." They all adjourned to the bar, where they had something at their host's expense. Then they repaired to his room, whence for the ensuing two hours the bell and the bell-boy were kept briskly going.

The gentleman from Alabama was in his glory. His gestures as he held forth were those of a gracious and condescending prince. It was his first visit to the city, and he said to the Washington man: "I tell you, sir, you've got a mighty fine town here. Of course, there's no opportunity for anything like local pride, because it's the outsiders, or the whole country, rather, that makes it what it is, but that's nothing. It's a fine town, and I'm right sorry that I can't stay longer."

"How long do you expect to be with us, Professor?" inquired Col. Mason, the horse who had bent his force to the party wheel in the Georgia ruts.

"Oh, about ten days, I reckon, at the furthest. I want to spend some time sight-seeing. I'll drop in on the Congressman from my district tomorrow, and call a little later on the President."

"Uh, huh!" said Col. Mason. He had been in the city for some time.

"Yes, sir, I want to get through with my little matter and get back home. I'm not asking for much, and I don't anticipate any trouble in securing what I desire. You see, it's just like this, there's no way for them to refuse us. And if any one deserves the good things at the hands of the administration, who more than we old campaigners, who have been helping the party through its fights from the time that we had our first votes?"

"Who, indeed?" said the Washington man.

"I tell you, gentlemen, the administration is no fool. It knows that we hold the colored vote down there in our vest pockets and it ain't going to turn us down."

"No, of course not, but sometimes there are delays——"

"Delays, to be sure, where a man doesn't know how to go about the matter. The thing to do, is to go right to the centre of authority at once. Don't you see?"

"Certainly, certainly," chorused the other gentlemen.

Before going, the Washington man suggested that the newcomer join them that evening and see something of society at the capital. "You know," he said, "that outside of New Orleans, Washington is

the only town in the country that has any colored society to speak
of, and I feel that you distinguished men from different sections of
the country owe it to our people that they should be allowed to see
you. It would be an inspiration to them."

So the matter was settled, and promptly at 8:30 o'clock Mr.
Cornelius Johnson joined his friends at the door of his hotel. The
grey Prince Albert was scrupulously buttoned about his form, and
a shiny top hat replaced the felt of the afternoon. Thus clad, he
went forth into society, where he need be followed only long
enough to note the magnificence of his manners and the enthusi-
asm of his reception when he was introduced as Prof. Cornelius
Johnson, of Alabama, in a tone which insinuated that he was the
only really great man his state had produced.

It might also be stated as an effect of this excursion into Vanity
Fair, that when he woke the next morning he was in some doubt as
to whether he should visit his Congressman or send for that individual to call upon him. He had felt the subtle flattery of attention
from that section of colored society which imitates—only imitates,
it is true, but better than any other, copies—the kindnesses and
cruelties, the niceties and deceits, of its white prototype. And for
the time, like a man in a fog, he had lost his sense of proportion
and perspective. But habit finally triumphed, and he called upon
the Congressman, only to be met by an under-secretary who told
him that his superior was too busy to see him that morning.

"But——"

"Too busy," repeated the secretary.

Mr. Johnson drew himself up and said: "Tell Congressman
Barker that Mr. Johnson, Mr. Cornelius Johnson, of Alabama,
desires to see him. I think he will see me."

"Well, I can take your message," said the clerk, doggedly, "but
I tell you now it won't do you any good. He won't see any one."

But, in a few moments an inner door opened, and the young
man came out followed by the desired one. Mr. Johnson couldn't
resist the temptation to let his eyes rest on the underling in a
momentary glance of triumph as Congressman Barker hurried up
to him, saying: "Why, why, Cornelius, how'do? how'do? Ah, you
came about that little matter, didn't you? Well, well, I haven't
forgotten you; I haven't forgotten you."

The colored man opened his mouth to speak, but the other
checked him and went on: "I'm sorry, but I'm in a great hurry
now. I'm compelled to leave town to-day, much against my will,

but I shall be back in a week; come around and see me then. Always glad to see you, you know. Sorry I'm so busy now; good-morning, good-morning."

Mr. Johnson allowed himself to be guided politely, but decidedly, to the door. The triumph died out of his face as the reluctant good-morning fell from his lips. As he walked away, he tried to look upon the matter philosophically. He tried to reason with himself—to prove to his own consciousness that the Congressman was very busy and could not give the time that morning. He wanted to make himself believe that he had not been slighted or treated with scant ceremony. But, try as he would, he continued to feel an obstinate, nasty sting that would not let him rest, nor forget his reception. His pride was hurt. The thought came to him to go at once to the President, but he had experience enough to know that such a visit would be vain until he had seen the dispenser of patronage for his district. Thus, there was nothing for him to do but to wait the necessary week. A whole week! His brow knitted as he thought of it.

In the course of these cogitations, his walk brought him to his hotel, where he found his friends of the night before awaiting him. He tried to put on a cheerful face. But his disappointment and humiliation showed through his smile, as the hollows and bones through the skin of a cadaver.

"Well, what luck?" asked Col. Mason, cheerfully.

"Are we to congratulate you?" put in Mr. Perry.

"Not yet, not yet, gentlemen. I have not seen the President yet. The fact is—ahem—my Congressman is out of town."

He was not used to evasions of this kind, and he stammered slightly and his yellow face turned brick-red with shame.

"It is most annoying," he went on, "most annoying. Mr. Barker won't be back for a week, and I don't want to call on the President until I have had a talk with him."

"Certainly not," said Col. Mason, blandly. "There will be delays." This was not his first pilgrimage to Mecca.

Mr. Johnson looked at him gratefully. "Oh, yes; of course, delays," he assented; "most natural. Have something."

At the end of the appointed time, the office-seeker went again to see the Congressman. This time he was admitted without question, and got the chance to state his wants. But somehow, there seemed to be innumerable obstacles in the way. There were certain other men whose wishes had to be consulted; the leader of one of the party factions, who, for the sake of harmony, had to be appeased. Of course, Mr. Johnson's worth was fully recognized, and he would be rewarded according to his deserts. His interests would be looked after. He should drop in again in a day or two. It took time, of course, it took time.

Mr. Johnson left the office unnerved by his disappointment. He had thought it would be easy to come up to Washington, claim and get what he wanted, and, after a glance at the town, hurry back to his home and his honors. It had all seemed so easy—before election; but now——

A vague doubt began to creep into his mind that turned him sick at heart. He knew how they had treated Davis, of Louisiana. He had heard how they had once kept Brotherton, of Texas—a man who had spent all his life in the service of his party—waiting clear through a whole administration, at the end of which the opposite party had come into power. All the stories of disappointment and disaster that he had ever heard came back to him, and he began to wonder if some one of these things was going to happen to him.

Every other day for the next two weeks, he called upon Barker, but always with the same result. Nothing was clear yet, until one day the bland legislator told him that considerations of expediency had compelled them to give the place he was asking for to another man.

"But what am I to do?" asked the helpless man.

"Oh, you just bide your time. I'll look out for you. Never fear."

Until now, Johnson had ignored the gentle hints of his friend, Col. Mason, about a boardinghouse being more convenient than a hotel. Now, he asked him if there was a room vacant where he was staying, and finding that there was, he had his things moved thither at once. He felt the change keenly, and although no one really paid any attention to it, he believed that all Washington must have seen it, and hailed it as the first step in his degradation.

For a while the two together made occasional excursions to a glittering palace down the street, but when the money had grown lower and lower Col. Mason had the knack of bringing "a little something" to their rooms without a loss of dignity. In fact, it was in these hours with the old man, over a pipe and a bit of something, that Johnson was most nearly cheerful. Hitch after hitch had occurred in his plans, and day after day he had come home unsuccessful and discouraged. The crowning disappointment, though, came when, after a long session that lasted even up into the hot days of summer, Congress adjourned and his one hope went away. Johnson saw him just before his departure, and listened ruefully as he said: "I tell you, Cornelius, now, you'd better go on home, get back to your business and come again next year. The clouds of battle will be somewhat dispelled by then and we can see clearer what to do. It was too early this year. We were too near the fight still, and there were party wounds to be bound up and little factional sores that had to be healed. But next year, Cornelius, next year we'll see what we can do for you."

His constituent did not tell him that even if his pride would let him go back home a disappointed applicant, he had not the means wherewith to go. He did not tell him that he was trying to keep up appearances and hide the truth from his wife, who, with their two children, waited and hoped for him at home.

When he went home that night, Col. Mason saw instantly that things had gone wrong with him. But here the tact and delicacy of the old politician came uppermost and, without trying to draw his story from him—for he already divined the situation too well—he sat for a long time telling the younger man stories of the ups and downs of men whom he had known in his long and active life.

They were stories of hardship, deprivation and discouragement. But the old man told them ever with a touch of cheeriness and the note of humor that took away the ghastly hopelessness of some of the pictures. He told them with such feeling and sympathy that Johnson was moved to frankness and told him his own pitiful tale.

Now that he had some one to whom he could open his heart, Johnson himself was no less willing to look the matter in the face, and even during the long summer days, when he had begun to live upon his wardrobe, piece by piece, he still kept up; although some of his pomposity went, along with the Prince Albert coat and the shiny hat. He now wore a shiny coat, and less showy head-gear. For a couple of weeks, too, he disappeared, and as he returned with some money, it was fair to presume that he had been at work somewhere, but he could not stay away from the city long.

It was nearing the middle of autumn when Col. Mason came home to their rooms one day to find his colleague more disheartened and depressed than he had ever seen him before. He was lying with his head upon his folded arm, and when he looked up there were traces of tears upon his face.

"Why, why, what's the matter now?" asked the old man. "No bad news, I hope."

"Nothing worse than I should have expected," was the choking answer. "It's a letter from my wife. She's sick and one of the babies is down, but"—his voice broke—"she tells me to stay and fight it out. My God, Mason, I could stand it if she whined or accused me or begged me to come home, but her patient, long-suffering bravery breaks me all up."

Col. Mason stood up and folded his arms across his big chest. "She's a brave little woman," he said, gravely. "I wish her husband was as brave a man." Johnson raised his head and arms from the table where they were sprawled, as the old man went on: "The hard conditions of life in our race have taught our women a patience and fortitude which the women of no other race have ever displayed. They have taught the men less, and I am sorry, very sorry. The thing, that as much as anything else, made the blacks such excellent soldiers in the civil war was their patient endurance of hardship. The softer education of more prosperous days seems to have weakened this quality. The man who quails or weakens in this fight of ours against adverse circumstances would have quailed before—no, he would have run from an enemy on the field."

"Why, Mason, your mood inspires me. I feel as if I could go forth to battle cheerfully." For the moment, Johnson's old pomposity had returned to him, but in the next, a wave of despondency bore it down. "But that's just it; a body feels as if he could fight if he only had something to fight. But here you strike out and hit—nothing. It's only a contest with time. It's waiting—waiting—waiting!"

"In this case, waiting is fighting."

"Well, even that granted, it matters not how grand his cause, the soldier needs his rations."

"Forage," shot forth the answer like a command.

"Ah, Mason, that's well enough in good country; but the army of office-seekers has devastated Washington. It has left a track as bare as lay behind Sherman's troopers." Johnson rose more cheerfully. "I'm going to the telegraph office," he said as he went out.

A few days after this, he was again in the best of spirits, for there was money in his pocket.

"What have you been doing?" asked Mr. Toliver.

His friend laughed like a boy. "Something very imprudent, I'm sure you will say. I've mortgaged my little place down home. It did not bring much, but I had to have money for the wife and the children, and to keep me until Congress assembles; then I believe that everything will be all right."

Col. Mason's brow clouded and he sighed.

On the reassembling of the two Houses, Congressman Barker was one of the first men in his seat. Mr. Cornelius Johnson went to see him soon.

"What, you here already, Cornelius?" asked the legislator.

"I haven't been away," was the answer.

"Well, you've got the hang-on, and that's what an office-seeker needs. Well, I'll attend to your matter among the very first. I'll visit the President in a day or two."

The listener's heart throbbed hard. After all his waiting, triumph was his at last.

He went home walking on air, and Col. Mason rejoiced with him. In a few days came word from Barker: "Your appointment was sent in to-day. I'll rush it through on the other side. Come up to-morrow afternoon."

Cornelius and Mr. Toliver hugged each other.

"It came just in time," said the younger man; "the last of my money was about gone, and I should have had to begin paying off that mortgage with no prospect of ever doing it."

The two had suffered together, and it was fitting that they should be together to receive the news of the long-desired happiness; so arm in arm they sauntered down to the Congressman's office about five o'clock the next afternoon. In honor of the occasion, Mr. Johnson had spent his last dollar in redeeming the grey Prince Albert and the shiny hat. A smile flashed across Barker's face as he noted the change.

"Well, Cornelius," he said, "I'm glad to see you still prosperous-looking, for there were some alleged irregularities in your methods down in Alabama, and the Senate has refused to confirm you. I did all I could for you, but——"

The rest of the sentence was lost, as Col. Mason's arms received his friend's fainting form.

"Poor devil!" said the Congressman. "I should have broken it more gently."

Somehow Col. Mason got him home and to bed, where for nine weeks he lay wasting under a complete nervous give-down. The little wife and the children came up to nurse him, and the woman's ready industry helped him to such creature comforts as his sickness demanded. Never once did she murmur; never once did her faith in him waver. And when he was well enough to be moved back, it was money that she had earned, increased by what Col. Mason, in his generosity of spirit, took from his own narrow means, that paid their second-class fare back to the South.

During the fever-fits of his illness, the wasted politician first begged piteously that they would not send him home unplaced, and then he would break out in the most extravagant and pompous boasts about his position, his Congressman and his influence.

When he came to himself, he was silent, morose, and bitter. Only once did he melt. It was when he held Col. Mason's hand and bade him good-bye. Then the tears came into his eyes, and what he would have said was lost among his broken words.

As he stood upon the platform of the car as it moved out, and gazed at the white dome and feathery spires of the city, growing into grey indefiniteness, he ground his teeth, and raising his spent hand, shook it at the receding view. "Damn you! damn you!" he cried. "Damn your deceit, your fair cruelties; damn you, you hard, white liar!"

Jean Toomer (1894-1967)

Fern

In 1923 Jean Toomer seemed destined to be a major American writer. His poems and stories were eagerly sought by editors, and he had received accolades from such writers and critics as Sherwood Anderson, Waldo Frank, Gorham Munson, and W. S. Braithwaite. Except for a privately printed collection of aphorisms, however, Jean Toomer published no books after 1923. He remains, therefore, an important but tragic figure in black American literature.

Born in Washington, D. C., Nathan Eugene Toomer was the grandson of P. B. S. Pinchback, who, during Reconstruction, served as Acting Governor of Louisiana. After enrolling briefly at the University of Wisconsin, the American School of Physical Education in Chicago, the University of Chicago, the City College of New York, and New York University, where he considered and rejected studies in agriculture, physical education, medicine, sociology, and history, Jean Toomer settled on a career as a writer, which he interrupted by accepting a position as acting principal in Sparta, Georgia, in the fall of 1922. Inspired with the belief that he had located his roots in the ancestral home of his people, Toomer wrote poems, stories, and sketches, especially about Southern women whose gropings for self-realization forced them into conflict with the dominant moral attitudes of American society. When he returned to Washington, he wrote stories, poems, and sketches about more inhibited black people in Washington and

---

From *Cane* (New York: Boni & Liveright, 1923). © 1923 by Boni & Liveright, Inc. Reprinted by permission of Liveright Publishers.

Chicago. He collected and published these as *Cane* (1923), a classic in black American literature.

Toomer's personal search for identity, however, did not end with *Cane*. A student of Eastern philosophies, he discovered a spiritual leader in George Gurdjieff and dedicated himself to teaching the Gurdjieffan ideas to the American people. In the process he smothered his lyricism under satire and didacticism by offering psychological case studies rather than sympathetic sketches. When publishers rejected these works, he accused them of restricting him to Negro subjects because they identified him as a Negro. Instead, he argued, he should be judged as an American rather than a Negro; subsequently, he even denied that he had any Negro ancestors. America refused to accept his attitudes about race. A weekly magazine made national scandal of his marriage to Caucasian Margery Latimer, a promising writer who had been his disciple in a Gurdjieffan experiment which the newspapers had characterized as a "free love" colony. Toomer attempted to answer his critics by writing novels about his marriage and about the Gurdieffan philosophy. Publishers continued to reject them. He succeeded only in publishing essays, in which he explained his belief that America would give birth to a new race—neither white nor black, but American.

The tragic death of his wife in childbirth, the Depression, and rejections by publishers turned the Thirties into a decade of tragedy relieved only by a second marriage. For the remainder of his life, Toomer searched for spiritual understanding through the Friends Society, psychiatry, and Indian mysticism. Occasionally he lectured to college students and to gatherings of the Friends. He continued to write plays, novels, poems, and stories; but, except for an occasional poem or story, his efforts went unpublished. He died in a rest home in 1967.

"Fern" reveals both the strengths and weaknesses of Toomer's early work. The style is lyric; the characterization is haunting; yet the piece is a sketch rather than a well-developed story.

Fern

Face flowed into her eyes. Flowed in soft cream foam and plaintive ripples, in such a way that wherever your glance may momentarily have rested it immediately thereafter wavered in the direction of her eyes. The soft suggestion of down slightly darkened, like the shadow of a bird's wing might, the creamy brown color of her upper lip. Why after noticing it you sought her eyes, I cannot tell you. Her nose was aquiline, Semitic. If you have heard a Jewish cantor sing, if he has touched you and made your own sorrow seem trivial when compared with his, you will know my feeling when I follow the curves of her profile, like mobile rivers, to their common delta. They were strange eyes. In this, that they sought nothing—that is, nothing that was obvious and tangible and that one could see, and they gave the impression that nothing was to be denied. When a woman seeks, you will have observed, her eyes deny. Fern's eyes desired nothing that you could give her; there was no reason why they should withhold. Men saw her eyes and fooled themselves. Fern's eyes said to them that she was easy. When she was young, a few men took her, but got no joy from it. And then, once done, they felt bound to her (quite unlike their hit and run with other girls), felt as though it would take them a lifetime to fulfill an obligation which they could find no name for. They became attached to her, and hungered after finding the barest trace of what she might desire. As she grew up, new men who came to town felt as almost everyone did who ever saw her: that they would not be denied. Men were everlastingly bringing her their bodies. Something inside of her got tired of them, I guess, for I am certain that for the life of her she could not tell why or how she began to turn them off. A man in fever is no trifling thing to send away. They began to leave her, baffled and ashamed, yet vowing to themselves that someday they would do some fine thing for her: send her candy every week and not let her know whom it came from, watch out for her wedding day and give her a magnificent something with no name on it, buy a house and deed it to her, rescue her from some unworthy fellow who had tricked her into marrying him. As you know, men are apt to idolize or fear that which they cannot understand, especially if it be a woman. She did not deny them, yet the fact was that they were denied. A sort of superstition crept into their consciousness of her being somehow above them. Being above them meant that she was not to be approached by anyone. She became a virgin. Now a virgin in a small Southern town is by no means the usual thing, if you will believe me. That the sexes were made to mate is the practice of the South. Particularly, black folks were made to mate. And it is black folks whom I have been talking about thus far. What white men thought of Fern I can arrive at only by analogy. They let her alone.

Anyone of course could see her, could see her eyes. If you walked up the Dixie Pike most any time of day, you'd be most like to see her resting listless-like on the railing of her porch, back propped against a post, head tilted a little forward because there was a nail in the porch post just where her head came which for some reason or other she never took the trouble to pull out. Her eyes, if it were sunset, rested idly where the sun, molten and glorious, was pouring down between the fringe of pines. Or maybe they gazed at the gray cabin on the knoll from which an evening folksong was coming. Perhaps they followed a cow that had been turned loose to roam and feed on cotton stalks and corn leaves. Like as not they'd settle on some vague spot above the horizon, though hardly a trace of wistfulness would come to them. If it were dusk, then they'd wait for the searchlight of the evening train which you could see miles up the track before it flared across the Dixie Pike, close to her home. Wherever they looked, you'd follow them and then waver back. Like her face, the whole countryside seemed to flow into her eyes. Flowed into them with the soft listless cadence of Georgia's South. A young Negro, once, was looking at her spellbound from the road. A white man passing in a buggy had to flick him with his whip if he was to get by without running him over. I first saw her on her porch. I was passing with a fellow whose crusty numbness (I was from the North and suspected of being prejudiced and stuck-up) was melting as he found me warm. I asked him who she was. "That's Fern," was all that I could get from him. Some folks already thought I was given to nosing around; I let it go at that, so far as questions were concerned. But at first sight of her I felt as if I heard a Jewish cantor sing. As if his singing rose above the unheard chorus of a folksong. And I felt bound to her. I too had my dreams: something I would do for her. I have knocked about from town to town too much not to know the futility of mere change of place. Besides, picture if you can this cream-colored solitary girl sitting at a tenement window looking down on the indifferent throngs of Harlem. Better that she listen to folksongs at dusk in Georgia, you would say, and so would I. Or suppose she came up North and married. Even a doctor or a lawyer, say, one who would be sure to get along—that is, make money. You and I know, who have had experience in such things, that love is not a thing like prejudice which can be bettered by changes of town. Could men in Washington, Chicago, or New York, more than the men of Georgia, bring her something left vacant by the bestowal of their bodies? You and I who know men

in these cities will have to say, they could not. See her out and out
a prostitute along State Street in Chicago. See her move into a
Southern town where white men are more aggressive. See her
become a white man's concubine. . . . Something I must do for her.
There was myself. What could I do for her? Talk, of course. Push
back the fringe of pines upon new horizons. To what purpose? and
what for? Her? Myself? Men in her case seem to lose their selfish-
ness. I lost mine before I touched her. I ask you, friend (it makes
no difference if you sit in the Pullman or the Jim Crow as the train
crosses her road), what thoughts would come to you—that is, after
you'd finished with the thoughts that leap into men's minds at the
sight of a pretty woman who will not deny them; what thoughts
would come to you, had you seen her in a quick flash, keen and
intuitively, as she sat there on her porch when your train thundered by? Would you have got off at the next station and come
back for her to take her, where? Would you have completely
forgotten her as soon as you reached Macon, Atlanta, Augusta,
Pasadena, Madison, Chicago, Boston, or New Orleans? Would you
tell your wife or sweetheart about a girl you saw? Your thoughts
can help me, and I would like to know. Something I would do for
her. . . .

One evening I walked up the Pike on purpose, and stopped to
say hello. Some of her family were about, but they moved away to
make room for me. Damn if I knew how to begin. Would you? Mr.
and Miss So-and-So, people, the weather, the crops, the new
preacher, the frolic, the church benefit, rabbit and possum hunting, the new soft drink they had at old Pap's store, the schedule
of the trains, what kind of town Macon was, Negro's migration
north, boll weevils, syrup, the Bible—to all these things she gave a
yassur or nassur, without further comment. I began to wonder if
perhaps my own emotional sensibility had played one of its tricks
on me. "Let's take a walk," I at last ventured. The suggestion,
coming after so long an isolation, was novel enough, I guess, to
surprise. But it wasn't that. Something told me that men before
me had said just that as a prelude to the offering of their bodies. I
tried to tell her with my eyes. I think she understood. The thing
from her that made my throat catch, vanished. Its passing left her
visible in a way I'd thought, but never seen. We walked down the
Pike with people on all the porches gaping at us. "Doesn't it make
you mad?" She meant the world. Through a canebrake that was
ripe for cutting, the branch was reached. Under a sweet-gum tree,
and where reddish leaves had dammed the creek a little, we sat

down. Dusk, suggesting the almost imperceptible procession of giant trees, settled with a purple haze about the cane. I felt strange, as I always do in Georgia, particularly at dusk. I felt that things unseen to men were tangibly immediate. It would not have surprised me had I had a vision. People have them in Georgia more often then you would suppose. A black woman once saw the mother of Christ and drew her in charcoal on the courthouse wall. . . . When one is on the soil of one's ancestors, most anything can come to one. . . . From force of habit, I suppose, I held Fern in my arms—that is, without at first noticing it. Then my mind came back to her. Her eyes, unusually weird and open, held me. Held God. He flowed in as I've seen the countryside flow in. Seen men. I must have done something—what, I don't know, in the confusion of my emotion. She sprang up. Rushed some distance from me. Fell to her knees, and began swaying, swaying. Her body was tortured with something it could not let out. Like boiling sap it flooded arms and fingers till she shook them as if they burned her. It found her throat, and spattered inarticulately in plaintive, convulsive sounds, mingled with calls to Christ Jesus. And then she sang, brokenly. A Jewish cantor singing with a broken voice. A child's voice, uncertain, or an old man's. Dusk hid her; I could hear only her song. It seemed to me as though she were pounding her head in anguish upon the ground. I rushed to her. She fainted in my arms.

There was talk about her fainting with me in the canefield. And I got one or two ugly looks from town men who'd set themselves up to protect her. In fact, there was talk of making me leave town. But they never did. They kept a watch out for me, though. Shortly after, I came back North. From the train window I saw her as I crossed her road. Saw her on her porch, head tilted a little forward where the nail was, eyes vaguely focused on the sunset. Saw her face flow into them, the countryside and something that I call God, flowing into them. . . . Nothing ever really happened. Nothing ever came to Fern, not even I. Something I would do for her. Some fine unnamed thing. . . . And, friend, you? She is still living, I have reason to know. Her name, against the chance that you might happen down that way, is Fernie May Rosen.

Wallace Thurman (1902-1934)

Cordelia the Crude

Born in Salt Lake City, Utah, and educated at the University of Southern California, Wallace Thurman was a leader among the young black intelligensia who earned their literary reputations during the Harlem Renaissance. A magazine writer and a member of the editorial staffs of *The Messenger* and the Macaulay Publishing Company, Thurman is best known to contemporary readers for *The Blacker the Berry* (1929), a novel examining the problem of a young woman who feels inferior and alienated because she has dark skin. In the same year Thurman collaborated with W. J. Rapp on *Harlem*, a play which ran briefly on Broadway. Two years before he died from tuberculosis, he wrote a second novel, *Infants of the Spring*, which satirizes black artists of the Twenties.

"Cordelia the Crude," taken from *Fire*, a short-lived periodical which Thurman helped found, is one of his earliest stories. It demonstrates the irony which he later sharpened in his novels.

Cordelia the Crude

Physically, if not mentally, Cordelia was a potential prostitute, meaning that although she had not yet realized the moral import of her wanton promiscuity nor become mercenary, she had, nevertheless, become quite blasé and bountiful in the matter of bestowing sexual favors upon persuasive and likely young men. Yet,

---

From *Fire*, I (November, 1926).

despite her seeming lack of discrimination, Cordelia was quite particular about the type of male to whom she submitted, for numbers do not necessarily denote a lack of taste, and Cordelia had discovered after several months of active observation that one could find the qualities one admires or reacts positively to in a varied hodge-podge of outwardly different individuals.

The scene of Cordelia's activities was The Roosevelt Motion Picture Theatre on Seventh Avenue near 145th Street. Thrice weekly the program changed, and thrice weekly Cordelia would plunk down the necessary twenty-five cents evening admission fee, and saunter gaily into the foul-smelling depths of her favorite cinema shrine. The Roosevelt Theatre presented all of the latest pictures, also, twice weekly, treated its audiences to a vaudeville bill, then too, one could always have the most delightly physical contacts . . . hmm. . . .

Cordelia had not consciously chosen this locale nor had there been any conscious effort upon her part to take advantage of the extra opportunities afforded for physical pleasure. It had just happened that the Roosevelt Theatre was more close to her home than any other neighborhood picture palace, and it had also just happened that Cordelia had become almost immediately initiated into the ways of a Harlem theatre chippie soon after her discovery of the theatre itself.

It is the custom of certain men and boys who frequent these places to idle up and down the aisle until some female is seen sitting alone, to slouch down into a seat beside her, to touch her foot or else press her leg in such a way that it can be construed as accidental if necessary, and then, if the female is wise or else shows signs of willingness to become wise, to make more obvious approaches until, if successful, the approached female will soon be chatting with her baiter about the picture being shown, lolling in his arms, and helping to formulate plans for an after-theatre rendezvous. Cordelia had, you see, shown a willingness to become wise upon her second visit to The Roosevelt. In a short while she had even learned how to squelch the bloated, lewd faced Jews and eager middle aged Negroes who might approach as well as how to inveigle the likeable little yellow or brown half men, embryo avenue sweetbacks, with their well modeled heads, stickily plastered hair, flaming cravats, silken or broadcloth shirts, dirty underwear, low cut vests, form fitting coats, bell-bottom trousers and shiny shoes with metal cornered heels clicking with a brave, brazen rhythm upon the bare concrete floor as their owners angled and searched for prey.

Cordelia, sixteen years old, matronly mature, was an undisciplined, half literate product of rustic South Carolina, and had come to Harlem very much against her will with her parents and her six brothers and sisters. Against her will because she had not been at all anxious to leave the lackadaisical life of the little corn pone settlement where she had been born, to go trooping into the unknown vastness of New York, for she had been in love, passionately in love with one John Stokes who raised pigs, and who, like his father before him, found the raising of pigs so profitable that he could not even consider leaving Lintonville. Cordelia had blankly informed her parents that she would not go with them when they decided to be lured to New York by an older son who had remained there after the demobilization of the war time troops. She had even threatened to run away with John until they should be gone, but of course John could not leave his pigs, and John's mother was not very keen on having Cordelia for a daughter-in-law—those Joneses have bad mixed blood in 'em—so Cordelia had had to join the Gotham bound caravan and leave her lover to his succulent porkers.

However, the mere moving to Harlem had not doused the rebellious flame. Upon arriving Cordelia had not only refused to go to school and refused to hold even the most easily held job, but had also victoriously defied her harassed parents so frequently when it came to matters of discipline that she soon found herself with a mesmerizing lack of home restraint, for the stress of trying to maintain themselves and their family in the new environment was far too much of a task for Mr. and Mrs. Jones to attend to facilely and at the same time try to control a recalcitrant child. So, when Cordelia had refused either to work or to attend school, Mrs. Jones herself had gone out for day's work, leaving Cordelia at home to take care of their five room railroad flat, the front room of which was rented out to a couple "living together," and to see that the younger children, all of whom were of school age, made their four trips daily between home and the nearby public school—as well as see that they had their greasy, if slim, food rations and an occasional change of clothing. Thus Cordelia's days were full—and so were her nights. The only difference being that the days belonged to the folks at home while the nights (since the folks were too tired or too sleepy to know or care when she came in or went

out) belonged to her and to—well—whosoever will, let them
come.

Cordelia had been playing this hectic, entrancing game for six
months and was widely known among a certain group of young
men and girls on the avenue as a fus' class chippie when she and I
happened to enter the theatre simultaneously. She had clumped
down the aisle before me, her open galoshes swishing noisily, her
two arms busy wriggling themselves free from the torn sleeve
lining of a shoddy imitation fur coat that one of her mother's wash
clients had sent to her. She was of medium height and build, with
overly developed legs and bust, and had a clear, keen light brown
complexion. Her too slick, too naturally bobbed hair, mussed by
the removing of a tight, black turban was of an undecided nature,
i.e., it was undecided whether to be kinky or to be kind, and her
body, as she sauntered along in the partial light had such a
conscious sway of invitation that unthinkingly I followed, slid into
the same row of seats and sat down beside her.

Naturally she had noticed my pursuit, and thinking that I was
eager to play the game, let me know immediately that she was
wise, and not the least bit averse to spooning with me during the
evening's performance. Interested, and, I might as well confess,
intrigued physically, I too became wise, and played up to her with
all the fervor, or so I thought, of an old timer, but Cordelia soon
remarked that I was different from mos' of des' sheiks, and when
pressed for an explanation brazenly told me in a slightly scandal-
ized and patronizing tone that I had not even felt her legs . . . !

At one o'clock in the morning we strolled through the snowy
bleakness of one hundred and forty-fourth street between Lenox
and Fifth Avenues to the walk-up tenement flat in which she lived,
and after stamping the snow from our feet, pushed through the
double outside doors, and followed the dismal hallway to the rear
of the building where we began the tedious climbing of the
crooked, creaking, inconveniently narrow stairway. Cordelia had
informed me earlier in the evening that she lived on the top
floor—four flights up east side rear—and on our way we rested at
each floor and at each halfway landing, rested long enough to
mingle the snowy dampness of our respective coats, and to hug
clumsily while our lips met in an animal kiss.

Finally only another half flight remained, and instead of pro-
ceeding as was usual after our amourous demonstration I abruptly
drew away from her, opened my overcoat, plunged my hand into
my pants pocket, and drew out two crumpled one dollar bills

which I handed to her, and then, while she stared at me foolishly, I muttered good-night, confusedly pecked her on her cold brown cheek, and darted down into the creaking darkness.

Six months later I was taking two friends of mine, lately from the provinces, to a Saturday night house-rent party in a well known whore house on one hundred and thirty-fourth street near Lenox Avenue. The place as we entered seemed to be a chaotic riot of raucous noise and clashing color all rhythmically merging in the red, smoke filled room. And there I saw Cordelia savagely careening in a drunken abortion of the Charleston and surrounded by a perspiring circle of handclapping enthusiasts. Finally fatigued, she whirled into an abrupt finish, and stopped so that she stared directly into my face, but being dizzy from the calisthenic turns and the cauterizing liquor she doubted that her eyes recognized someone out of the past, and, visibly trying to sober herself, languidly began to dance a slow drag with a lean hipped pimply faced yellow man who had walked between her and me. At last he released her, and seeing that she was about to leave the room I rushed forward calling Cordelia?—as if I was not yet sure who it was. Stopping in the doorway, she turned to see who had called, and finally recognizing me said simply, without the least trace of emotion—'Lo kid. . . .

And without another word turned her back and walked into the hall to where she joined four girls standing there. Still eager to speak, I followed and heard one of the girls ask: Who's the dicty kid? . . .

And Cordelia answered: The guy who gimme ma' firs' two bucks. . . .

Zora Neale Hurston (1903-1958)

Sweat

During her lifetime, Zora Neale Hurston earned respect both as a novelist and as a folklorist. Born in the all-Negro town of Eatonville, Florida, she worked as a maid and waitress and attended Morgan College and Howard University before earning a degree at Barnard, where she studied anthropology under Franz Boas while serving as personal secretary for Fannie Hurst. Supported by research grants, Miss Hurston collected Negro folklore in Florida, Louisiana, and, later, in Haiti and other parts of the Caribbean. Thus, she became the first black writer since Charles Chesnutt to give attention to the literary and cultural importance of folk material.

During the 1920's Miss Hurston began writing short stories about Southern Negroes, but she did not gain national prominence until the Thirties, when she published *Jonah's Gourd Vine* (1934), *Mules and Men* (1935), *Their Eyes Were Watching God* (1937), *Tell My Horse* (1938), and *Moses, Man of the Mountain* (1939). *Jonah's Gourd Vine* and *Their Eyes Were Watching God* are novels about Southern Negroes relatively unaffected by interracial conflicts. *Moses*, a satirical novel, draws delightful analogues between black Americans and "The Hebrew Children." *Mules and Men* and *Tell My Horse* are collections of folklore. After a long silence, Miss Hurston published her final novel, *Seraph in the Suwanee* (1948). When she died, she was reported to be working on another novel with a Biblical setting.

From *Fire,* I (November, 1926).

"Sweat," one of her first stories, reveals three major emphases of her work: skill in presenting the picturesque idiom of Southern Negroes, credible characterization, and her absorption with love and hatred in intrafamilial relationships. In her fiction, men and women love each other totally, or they hate vengefully.

Sweat

It was eleven o'clock of a Spring night in Florida. It was Sunday. Any other night, Delia Jones would have been in bed for two hours by this time. But she was a washwoman, and Monday morning meant a great deal to her. So she collected the soiled clothes on Saturday when she returned the clean things. Sunday night after church, she sorted them and put the white things to soak. It saved her almost a half day's start. A great hamper in the bedroom held the clothes that she brought home. It was so much neater than a number of bundles lying around.

She squatted in the kitchen floor beside the great pile of clothes, sorting them into small heaps according to color, and humming a song in a mournful key, but wondering through it all where Sykes, her husband, had gone with her horse and buckboard.

Just then something long, round, limp and black fell upon her shoulders and slithered to the floor beside her. A great terror took hold of her. It softened her knees and dried her mouth so that it was a full minute before she could cry out or move. Then she saw that it was the big bull whip her husband liked to carry when he drove.

She lifted her eyes to the door and saw him standing there bent over with laughter at her fright. She screamed at him.

"Sykes, what you throw dat whip on me like dat? You know it would skeer me—looks just like a snake, an' you knows how skeered Ah is of snakes."

"Course Ah knowed it! That's how come Ah done it." He slapped his leg with his hand and almost rolled on the ground in his mirth. "If you such a big fool dat you got to have a fit over a earth worm or a string, Ah don't keer how bad Ah skeer you."

"You aint got no business doing it. Gawd knows it's a sin. Some day Ah'm gointuh drop dead from some of yo' foolishness. 'Nother thing, where you been wid mah rig? Ah feeds dat pony. He aint fuh you to be drivin' wid no bull whip."

"You sho is one aggravatin' nigger woman!" he declared and stepped into the room. She resumed her work and did not answer him at once. "Ah done tole you time and again to keep them white folks' clothes outa dis house."

He picked up the whip and glared down at her. Delia went on with her work. She went out into the yard and returned with a galvanized tub and set it on the washbench. She saw that Sykes had kicked all of the clothes together again, and now stood in her way truculently, his whole manner hoping, *praying*, for an argument. But she walked calmly around him and commenced to re-sort the things.

"Next time, Ah'm gointer kick 'em outdoors," he threatened as he struck a match along the leg of his corduroy breeches.

Delia never looked up from her work, and her thin, stooped shoulders sagged further.

"Ah aint for no fuss t'night Sykes. Ah just come from taking sacrament at the church house."

He snorted scornfully. "Yeah, you just come from de church house on a Sunday night, but heah you is gone to work on them clothes. You ain't nothing but a hypocrite. One of them amen-corner Christians—sing, whoop, and shout, then come home and wash white folks clothes on the Sabbath."

He stepped roughly upon the whitest pile of things, kicking them helter-skelter as he crossed the room. His wife gave a little scream of dismay, and quickly gathered them together again.

"Sykes, you quit grindin' dirt into these clothes! How can Ah git through by Sat'day if Ah don't start on Sunday?"

"Ah don't keer if you never git through. Anyhow, Ah done promised Gawd and a couple of other men, Ah aint gointer have it in mah house. Don't gimme no lip neither, else Ah'll throw 'em out and put mah fist up side yo' head to boot."

Delia's habitual meekness seemed to slip from her shoulders like a blown scarf. She was on her feet; her poor little body, her bare knuckly hands bravely defying the strapping hulk before her.

"Looka heah, Sykes, you done gone too fur. Ah been married to you fur fifteen years, and Ah been takin' in washin' fur fifteen years. Sweat, sweat, sweat! Work and sweat, cry and sweat, pray and sweat!"

"What's that got to do with me?" he asked brutally.

"What's it got to do with you, Sykes? Mah tub of suds is filled yo' belly with vittles more times than yo' hands is filled it. Mah sweat is done paid for this house and Ah reckon Ah kin keep on sweatin' in it."

She seized the iron skillet from the stove and struck a defensive pose, which act surprised him greatly, coming from her. It cowed him and he did not strike her as he usually did.

"Naw you won't," she panted, "that ole snaggle-toothed black woman you runnin' with aint comin' heah to pile up on *mah* sweat and blood. You aint paid for nothin' on this place, and Ah'm gointer stay right heah till Ah'm toted out foot foremost."

"Well, you better quit gittin' me riled up, else they'll be totin' you out sooner than you expect. Ah'm so tired of you Ah don't know whut to do. Gawd! how Ah hates skinny wimmen!"

A little awed by this new Delia, he sidled out of the door and slammed the back gate after him. He did not say where he had gone, but she knew too well. She knew very well that he would not return until nearly daybreak also. Her work over, she went on to bed but not to sleep at once. Things had come to a pretty pass!

She lay awake, gazing upon the debris that cluttered their matrimonial trail. Not an image left standing along the way. Anything like flowers had long ago been drowned in the salty stream that had been pressed from her heart. Her tears, her sweat, her blood. She had brought love to the union and he had brought a longing after the flesh. Two months after the wedding, he had given her the first brutal beating. She had the memory of his numerous trips to Orlando with all of his wages when he had returned to her penniless, even before the first year had passed. She was young and soft then, but now she thought of her knotty, muscles limbs, her harsh knuckly hands, and drew herself up into an unhappy little ball in the middle of the big feather bed. Too late now to hope for love, even if it were not Bertha it would be someone else. This case differed from the others only in that she was bolder than the others. Too late for everything except her little home. She had built it for her old days, and planted one by one the trees and flowers there. It was lovely to her, lovely.

Somehow, before sleep came, she found herself saying aloud: "Oh well, whatever goes over the Devil's back, is got to come under his belly. Sometime or ruther, Sykes, like everybody else, is gointer reap his sowing." After that she was able to build a spiritual earthworks against her husband. His shells could no longer reach her. *Amen.* She went to sleep and slept until he announced his presence in bed by kicking her feet and rudely snatching the cover away.

"Gimme some kivah heah, an' git yo' damn foots over on yo' own side! Ah oughter mash you in yo' mouf fuh drawing dat skillet on me."

Delia went clear to the rail without answering him. A triumphant indifference to all that he was or did.

The week was as full of work for Delia as all other weeks, and Saturday found her behind her little pony, collecting and delivering clothes.

It was a hot, hot day near the end of July. The village men on Joe Clarke's porch even chewed cane listlessly. They did not hurl the cane-knots as usual. They let them dribble over the edge of the porch. Even conversation had collapsed under the heat.

"Heah come Delia Jones," Jim Merchant said, as the shaggy pony came 'round the bend of the road toward them. The rusty buckboard was heaped with baskets of crisp, clean laundry.

"Yep," Joe Lindsay agreed. "Hot or col', rain or shine, jes ez reg'lar ez de weeks roll roun' Delia carries 'em an' fetches 'em on Sat'day."

"She better if she wanter eat," said Moss. "Syke Jones aint wuth de shot an' powder hit would tek tuh kill 'em. Not to *huh* he aint."

"He sho' aint," Walter Thomas chimed in. "It's too bad, too, cause she wuz a right pritty lil trick when he got huh. Ah'd uh mah'ied huh mahseff if he hadnter beat me to it."

Delia nodded briefly at the men as she drove past.

"Too much knockin' will ruin *any* 'oman. He done beat huh 'nough tuh kill three women, let 'lone change they looks," said Elijah Moseley. "How Syke kin stommuck dat big black greasy Mogul he's layin' roun' wid, gits me. Ah swear dat eight-rock couldn't kiss a sardine can Ah done thowed out de back do' 'way las' yeah."

"Aw, she's fat, thass how come. He's allus been crazy 'bout fat women," put in Merchant. "He'd a' been tied up wid one long time ago if he could a' found one tuh have him. Did Ah tell yuh 'bout him come sidlin' roun' *mah* wife—bringin' her a basket uh pecans outa his yard fuh a present? Yessir, mah wife! She tol' him tuh take 'em right straight back home, cause Delia works so hard

ovah dat washtub she reckon everything on de place taste lak
sweat an' soapsuds. Ah jus' wisht Ah'd a' caught 'im 'roun' dere!
Ah'd a' made his hips ketch on fiah down dat shell road."

"Ah know he done it, too. Ah sees 'im grinnin' at every 'oman
dat passes," Walter Thomas said. "But even so, he useter eat some
mighty big hunks uh humble pie tuh git dat lil' 'oman he got. She
wuz ez pritty ez a speckled pup! Dat wuz fifteen yeahs ago. He
useter be so skeered uh losin' huh, she could make him do some
parts of a husband's duty. Dey never wuz de same in de mind."

"There oughter be a law about him," said Lindsay. "He aint fit
tuh carry guts tuh a bear."

Clarke spoke for the first time. "Taint no law on earth dat kin
make a man be decent if it aint in 'im. There's plenty men dat
takes a wife lak dey do a joint uh sugar-cane. It's round, juicy an'
sweet when dey gits it. But dey squeeze an' grind, squeeze an'
grind an' wring tell dey wring every drop uh pleasure dat's in 'em
out. When dey's satisfied dat dey is wrung dry, dey treats 'em jes
lak dey do a cane-chew. Dey thows 'em away. Dey knows whut
dey is doin' while dey is at it, an' hates theirselves fuh it but they
keeps on hangin' after huh tell she's empty. Den dey hates huh fuh
bein' a cane-chew an' in de way."

"We oughter take Syke an' dat stray 'oman uh his'n down in
Lake Howell swamp an' lay on de rawhide till they cain't say
'Lawd a' mussy.' He allus wuz uh ovahbearin' niggah, but since
dat white 'oman from up north done teached 'im how to run a
automobile, he done got too biggety to live—an' we oughter kill
'im," Old Man Anderson advised.

A grunt of approval went around the porch. But the heat was
melting their civic virtue and Elijah Moseley began to bait Joe
Clarke.

"Come on, Joe, git a melon outa dere an' slice it up for yo'
customers. We'se all sufferin' wid de heat. De bear's done got *me!*"

"Thass right, Joe, a watermelon is jes' whut Ah needs tuh cure
de eppizudicks," Walter Thomas joined forces with Moseley.
"Come on dere, Joe. We all is steady customers an' you aint set us
up in a long time. Ah chooses dat long, bowlegged Floridy favorite."

"A god, an' be dough. You all gimme twenty cents and slice
away," Clarke retorted. "Ah needs a col' slice m'self. Heah, everybody chip in. Ah'll lend y'll mah meat knife."

The money was quickly subscribed and the huge melon brought
forth. At that moment, Sykes and Bertha arrived. A determined
silence fell on the porch and the melon was put away again.

Merchant snapped down the blade of his jackknife and moved toward the store door.

"Come on in, Joe, an' gimme a slab uh sow belly an' uh pound uh coffee—almost fuhgot 'twas Sat'day. Got to git on home." Most of the men left also.

Just then Delia drove past on her way home, as Sykes was ordering magnificently for Bertha. It pleased him for Delia to see.

"Git whutsoever yo' heart desires, Honey. Wait a minute, Joe. Give huh two botles uh strawberry soda-water, uh quart uh parched ground-peas, an' a block uh chewin' gum."

With all this they left the store, with Sykes reminding Bertha that this was his town and she could have it if she wanted it.

The men returned soon after they left, and held their watermelon feast.

"Where did Syke Jones git da 'oman from nohow?" Lindsay asked.

"Ovah Apopka. Guess dey musta been cleanin' out de town when she lef'. She don't look lak a thing but a hunk uh liver wid hair on it."

"Well, she sho' kin squall," Dave Carter contributed. "When she gits ready tuh laff, she jes' opens huh mouf an' latches it back tuh de las' notch. No ole grandpa alligator down in Lake Bell ain't got nothin' on huh."

Bertha had been in town three months now. Sykes was still paying her room rent at Della Lewis'—the only house in town that would have taken her in. Sykes took her frequently to Winter Park to "stomps." He still assured her that he was the swellest man in the state.

"Sho' you kin have dat lil' ole house soon's Ah kin git dat 'oman outa dere. Everything b'longs tuh me an' you sho' kin have it. Ah sho' 'bominates uh skinny 'oman. Lawdy, you sho' is got one portly shape on you! You kin git *anything* you wants. Dis is *mah* town an' you sho' kin have it."

Delia's work-worn knees crawled over the earth in Gethsemane and up the rocks of Calvary many, many times during these months. She avoided the villagers and meeting places in her efforts to be blind and deaf. But Bertha nullified this to a degree, by coming to Delia's house to call Sykes out to her at the gate.

Delia and Sykes fought all the time now with no peaceful interludes. They slept and ate in silence. Two or three times Delia had attempted a timid friendliness, but she was repulsed each time. It was plain that the breaches must remain agape.

The sun had burned July to August. The heat streamed down like a million hot arrows, smiting all things living upon the earth. Grass withered, leaves browned, snakes went blind in shedding and men and dogs went mad. Dog days!

Delia came home one day and found Sykes there before her. She wondered, but started to go on into the house without speaking, even though he was standing in the kitchen door and she must either stoop under his arm or ask him to move. He made no room for her. She noticed a soap box beside the steps, but paid no particular attention to it, knowing that he must have brought it there. As she was stooping to pass under his outstretched arm, he suddenly pushed her backward, laughingly.

"Look in de box dere Delia, Ah done brung yuh somethin'!"

She nearly fell upon the box in her stumbling, and when she saw what it held, she all but fainted outright.

"Syke! Syke, mah Gawd! You take dat rattlesnake 'way from heah! You *gottuh*. Oh, Jesus, have mussy!"

"Ah aint gut tuh do nuthin' uh de kin'—fact is Ah aint got tuh do nothin' but die. Taint no use uh you puttin' on airs makin' out lak you skeered uh dat snake—he's gointer stay right heah tell he die. He wouldn't bite me cause Ah knows how tuh handle 'im. Nohow he wouldn't risk breakin' out his fangs 'gin *yo'* skinny laigs."

"Naw, now Syke, don't keep dat thing 'roun' heah tuh skeer me tuh death. You knows Ah'm even feared uh earth worms. Thass de biggest snake Ah evah did see. Kill 'im Syke, please."

"Doan ast me tuh do nothin' fuh yuh. Goin' 'roun' tryin' tuh be so damn asterperious. Naw, Ah aint gonna kill it. Ah think uh damn sight mo' uh him dan you! Dat's a nice snake an' anybody doan lak 'im kin jes' hit de grit."

The village soon heard that Sykes had the snake, and came to see and ask questions.

"How de hen-fire did you ketch dat six-foot rattler, Syke?" Thomas asked.

"He's full uh frogs so he caint hardly move, thass how Ah eased up on 'm. But Ah'm a snake charmer an' knows how tuh handle 'em. Shux, dat aint nothin'. Ah could ketch one eve'y day if Ah so wanted tuh."

"Whut he needs is a heavy hick'ry club leaned real heavy on his head. Dat's de bes 'way tuh charm a rattlesnake."

"Naw, Walt, y'll jes' don't understand dese diamon' backs lak Ah do," said Sykes in a superior tone of voice.

The village agreed with Walter, but the snake stayed on. His box remained by the kitchen door with its screen wire covering. Two or three days later it had digested its meal of frogs and literally came to life. It rattled at every movement in the kitchen or the yard. One day as Delia came down the kitchen steps she saw his chalky-white fangs curved like scimitars hung in the wire meshes. This time she did not run away with averted eyes as usual. She stood for a long time in the doorway in a red fury that grew bloodier for every second that she regarded the creature that was her torment.

That night she broached the subject as soon as Sykes sat down to the table.

"Syke, Ah wants you tuh take dat snake 'way fum heah. You done starved me an' Ah put up widcher, you done beat me an Ah took dat, but you done kilt all mah insides bringin' dat varmint heah."

Sykes poured out a saucer full of coffee and drank it deliberately before he answered her.

"A whole lot Ah keer 'bout how you feels inside uh out. Dat snake aint goin' no damn wheah till Ah gits ready fuh 'im tuh go. So fur as beatin' is concerned, yuh aint took near all dat you gointer take ef yuh stay 'roun' *me*."

Delia pushed back her plate and got up from the table. "Ah hates you, Sykes," she said calmly. "Ah hates you tuh de same degree dat Ah useter love yuh. Ah done took an' took till mah belly is full up tuh mah neck. Dat's de reason Ah got mah letter fum de church an' moved mah membership tuh Woodbridge—so Ah don't haftuh take no sacrament wid yuh. Ah don't wantuh see yuh 'roun' me atall. Lay 'roun' wid dat 'oman all yuh wants tuh, but gwan 'way fum me an' mah house. Ah hates yuh lak uh suck-egg dog."

Sykes almost let the huge wad of corn bread and collard greens he was chewing fall out of his mouth in amazement. He had a hard time whipping himself up to the proper fury to try to answer Delia.

"Well, Ah'm glad you does hate me. Ah'm sho' tiahed uh you hangin' ontuh me. Ah don't want yuh. Look at yuh stringey ole neck! Yo' rawbony laigs an' arms is enough tuh cut uh man tuh death. You looks jes' lak de devvul's doll-baby tuh *me*. You cain't hate me no worse dan Ah hates you. Ah been hatin' *you* fuh years.

"Yo' ole black hide don't look lak nothin' tuh me, but uh passle uh wrinkled up rubber, wid yo' big ole yeahs flappin' on each side

lak up paih uh buzzard wings. Don't think Ah'm gointuh be run
'way fum mah house neither. Ah'm goin' tuh de white folks bout
you, mah young man, de very nex' time you lay yo' han's on me.
Mah cup is done run ovah." Delia said this with no signs of fear
and Sykes departed from the house, threatening her, but made not
the slightest move to carry out any of them.

That night he did not return at all, and the next day being
Sunday, Delia was glad she did not have to quarrel before she
hitched up her pony and drove the four miles to Woodbridge.

She stayed to the night service—"love feast"—which was very
warm and full of spirit. In the emotional winds her domestic trials
were borne far and wide so that she sang as she drove homeward,

> *"Jurden water, black an' col'*
> *Chills de body, not de soul*
> *An' Ah wantah cross Jurden in uh calm time."*

She came from the barn to the kitchen door and stopped.

"Whut's de mattah, ol' satan, you aint kickin' up yo' racket?"
She addressed the snake's box. Complete silence. She went on into
the house with a new hope in its birth struggles. Perhaps her
threat to go to the white folks had frightened Sykes! Perhaps he
was sorry! Fifteen years of misery and suppression had brought
Delia to the place where she would hope *anything* that looked
towards a way over or through her wall of inhibitions.

She felt in the match safe behind the stove at once for a match.
There was only one there.

"Dat niggah wouldn't fetch nothin' heah tuh save his rotten
neck, but he kin run thew whut Ah brings quick enough. Now he
done toted off nigh on tuh haff uh box uh matches. He done had
dat 'oman heah in mah house, too."

Nobody but a woman could tell how she knew this even before
she struck the match. But she did and it put her into a new fury.

Presently she brought in the tubs to put the white things to
soak. This time she decided she need not bring the hamper out of
the bedroom; she would go in there and do the sorting. She picked
up the pot-bellied lamp and went in. The room was small and the
hamper stood hard by the foot of the white iron bed. She could sit
and reach through the bedposts—resting as she worked.

"Ah wantah cross Jurden in uh calm time." She was singing
again. The mood of the "love feast" had returned. She threw back
the lid of the basket almost gaily. Then, moved by both horror and

terror, she sprang back toward the door. *There lay the snake in the basket!* He moved sluggishly at first, but even as she turned round and round, jumped up and down in an insanity of fear, he began to stir vigorously. She saw him pouring his awful beauty from the basket upon the bed, then she seized the lamp and ran as fast as she could to the kitchen. The wind from the open door blew out the light and the darkness added to her terror. She sped to the darkness of the yard, slamming the door after her before she thought to set down the lamp. She did not feel safe even on the ground, so she climbed up in the hay barn.

There for an hour or more she lay sprawled upon the hay a gibbering wreck.

Finally she grew quiet, and after that, coherent thought. With this, stalked through her a cold, bloody rage. Hours of this. A period of introspection, a space of retrospection, then a mixture of both. Out of this an awful calm.

"Well, Ah done de bes' Ah could. If things aint right, Gawd knows taint mah fault."

She went to sleep—a twitchy sleep—and woke up to a faint gray sky. There was a loud hollow sound below. She peered out. Sykes was at the wood-pile, demolishing a wire-covered box.

He hurried to the kitchen door, but hung outside there some minutes before he entered, and stood some minutes more inside before he closed it after him.

The gray in the sky was spreading. Delia descended without fear now, and crouched beneath the low bedroom window. The drawn shade shut out the dawn, shut in the night. But the thin walls held back no sound.

"Dat ol' scratch is woke up now!" She mused at the tremendous whirr inside, which every woodsman knows, is one of the sound illusions. The rattler is a ventriloquist. His whirr sounds to the right, to the left, straight ahead, behind, close under foot—everywhere but where it is. Woe to him who guesses wrong unless he is prepared to hold up his end of the argument! Sometimes he strikes without rattling at all.

Inside, Sykes heard nothing until he knocked a pot lid off the stove while trying to reach the match safe in the dark. He had emptied his pockets at Bertha's.

The snake seemed to wake up under the stove and Sykes made a quick leap into the bedroom. In spite of the gin he had had, his head was clearing now.

"Mah Gawd!" he chattered, "ef Ah could on'y strack uh light!"

The rattling ceased for a moment as he stood paralyzed. He waited. It seemed that the snake waited also.

"Oh, fuh de light! Ah thought he'd be too sick"—Sykes was muttering to himself when the whirr began again, closer, right underfoot this time. Long before this, Sykes' ability to think had been flattened down to primitive instinct and he leaped—onto the bed.

Outside Delia heard a cry that might have come from a maddened chimpanzee, a stricken gorilla. All the terror, all the horror, all the rage that man possibly could express, without a recognizable human sound.

A tremendous stir inside there, another series of animal screams, the intermittent whirr of the reptile. The shade torn violently down from the window, letting in the red dawn, a huge brown hand seizing the window stick, great dull blows upon the wooden floor punctuating the gibberish of sound long after the rattle of the snake had abruptly subsided. All this Delia could see and hear from her place beneath the window, and it made her ill. She crept over to the four-o'clocks and stretched herself on the cool earth to recover.

She lay there. "Delia, Delia!" She could hear Sykes calling in a most despairing tone as one who expected no answer. The sun crept on up, and he called. Delia could not move—her legs were gone flabby. She never moved, he called, and the sun kept rising.

"Mah Gawd!" She heard him moan, "Mah Gawd fum Heben!" She heard him stumbling about and got up from her flower-bed. The sun was growing warm. As she approached the door she heard him call out hopefully, "Delia, is dat you Ah heah?"

She saw him on his hands and knees as soon as she reached the door. He crept an inch or two toward her—all that he was able, and she saw his horribly swollen neck and his one open eye shining with hope. A surge of pity too strong to support bore her away from that eye that must, could not, fail to see the tubs. He would see the lamp. Orlando with its doctors was too far. She could scarcely reach the Chinaberry tree, where she waited in the growing heat while inside she knew the cold river was creeping up and up to extinguish that eye which must know by now that she knew.

(James) Langston Hughes
(1902-1967)

Thank You, M'am, Last Whipping
and Christmas Song

Langston Hughes was the most versatile and most productive Afro-American writer who ever lived. He wrote poetry, novels, plays, histories, librettos, short stories, a novel, and an opera. He edited collections of folklore, humor, and poetry.

Born in Joplin, Missouri, reared in Kansas and Ohio, Hughes traveled widely before he returned to America to earn a B.A. from Lincoln University (Pa.). After college he resumed the writing career which he had begun earlier.

Despite his frequent awards he never enjoyed the critical acclaim which came to such contemporaries as Countee Cullen, Richard Wright, and, later, James Baldwin and Ralph Ellison. But, in a forty-five year literary career he contributed significantly to black American literature. In his early poetry he was known for his experiments with jazz and blues rhythms. Forty years later, in *Montage of a Dream Deferred*, he was still experimenting—with the rhythm and idiom of a new generation. Continually interested in the theatre, he established several Negro theatrical groups and wrote a play, *Mulatto* (1934), which ran longer on Broadway than any Negro drama except *A Raisin in the Sun*.

He was not only concerned with diminishing bigotry in the world; he also wanted to arouse black Americans to more intense pride in themselves and in their cultural heritage. For this reason, he traveled extensively on the Negro college circuit reading his poetry to the younger generations; and he anthologized and described the literary and musical achievements of black men in all parts of the world.

Hughes's most significant contribution to American literature, however, is his creation of the stories and sketches about Jesse B. Semple. A Virginian transplanted in Harlem, Jesse B. Semple is a folk hero. Intelligent despite his lack of formal education, proud to be American, and glad to be alive, "Simple" lives and speaks for the ordinary black man.

The first of the following pieces is a story from his early period. The last two are Simple sketches.

Thank You, M'am

She was a large woman with a large purse that had everything in it but a hammer and nails. It had a long strap, and she carried it slung across her shoulder. It was about eleven o'clock at night, dark, and she was walking alone, when a boy ran up behind her and tried to snatch her purse. The strap broke with the sudden single tug the boy gave it from behind. But the boy's weight and the weight of the purse combined caused him to lose his balance. Instead of taking off full blast as he had hoped, the boy fell on his back on the sidewalk and his legs flew up. The large woman simply turned around and kicked him right square in his blue-jeaned sitter. Then she reached down, picked the boy up by his shirt front, and shook him until his teeth rattled.

After that the woman said, "Pick up my pocketbook, boy, and give it here."

She still held him tightly. But she bent down enough to permit him to stoop and pick up her purse. Then she said, "Now ain't you ashamed of yourself?"

Firmly gripped by his shirt front, the boy said, "Yes'm."

The woman said, "What did you want to do it for?"

The boy said, "I didn't aim to."

She said, "You a lie!"

By that time two or three people passed, stopped, turned to look, and some stood watching.

"If I turn you loose, will you run?" asked the woman.

"Yes'm," said the boy.

"Then I won't turn you loose," said the woman. She did not release him.

"Lady, I'm sorry," whispered the boy.

"Um-hum! Your face is dirty. I got a great mind to wash your face for you. Ain't you got nobody home to tell you to wash your face?"

"No'm," said the boy.

"Then it will get washed this evening," said the large woman, starting up the street, dragging the frightened boy behind her.

He looked as if he were fourteen or fifteen, frail and willow-wild, in tennis shoes and blue jeans.

The woman said, "You ought to be my son. I would teach you right from wrong. Least I can do right now is to wash your face. Are you hungry?"

"No'm," said the being-dragged boy. "I just want you to turn me loose."

"Was I bothering *you* when I turned that corner?" asked the woman.

"No'm."

"But you put yourself in contact with *me*," said the woman. "If you think that that contact is not going to last awhile, you got another thought coming. When I get through with you, sir, you are going to remember Mrs. Luella Bates Washington Jones."

Sweat popped out on the boy's face and he began to struggle. Mrs. Jones stopped, jerked him around in front of her, put a half nelson about his neck, and continued to drag him up the street. When she got to her door, she dragged the boy inside, down a hall, and into a large kitchenette-furnished room at the rear of the house. She switched on the light and left the door open. The boy could hear other roomers laughing and talking in the large house. Some of their doors were open, too, so he knew he and the woman were not alone. The woman still had him by the neck in the middle of her room.

She said, "What is your name?"

"Roger," answered the boy.

"Then, Roger, you go to that sink and wash your face," said the woman, whereupon she turned him loose—at last. Roger looked at the door—looked at the woman—looked at the door—*and went to the sink.*

"Let the water run until it gets warm," she said. "Here's a clean towel."

"You gonna take me to jail?" asked the boy, bending over the sink.

"Not with that face, I would not take you nowhere," said the woman. "Here I am trying to get home to cook me a bite to eat, and you snatch my pocketbook! Maybe you ain't been to your supper either, late as it be. Have you?"

"There's nobody home at my house," said the boy.

"Then we'll eat," said the woman. "I believe you're hungry—or been hungry—to try to snatch my pocketbook!"

"I want a pair of blue suede shoes," said the boy.

"Well, you didn't have to snatch *my* pocketbook to get some suede shoes," said Mrs. Luella Bates Washington Jones. "You could of asked me."

"M'am?"

The water dripping from his face, the boy looked at her. There was a long pause. A very long pause. After he had dried his face, and not knowing what else to do, dried it again, the boy turned around, wondering what next. The door was open. He could make a dash for it down the hall. He could run, run, run, *run!*

The woman was sitting on the daybed. After a while she said, "I were young once and I wanted things I could not get."

There was another long pause. The boy's mouth opened. Then he frowned, not knowing he frowned.

The woman said, "Um-hum! You thought I was going to say *but,* didn't you? You thought I was going to say, *but I didn't snatch people's pocketbooks.* Well, I wasn't going to say that." Pause. Silence. "I have done things, too, which I would not tell you, son—neither tell God, if He didn't already know. Everybody's got something in common. So you set down while I fix us something to eat. You might run that comb through your hair so you will look presentable."

In another corner of the room behind a screen was a gas plate and an icebox. Mrs. Jones got up and went behind the screen. The woman did not watch the boy to see if he was going to run now, nor did she watch her purse, which she left behind her on the daybed. But the boy took care to sit on the far side of the room, away from the purse, where he thought she could easily see him out of the corner of her eye if she wanted to. He did not trust the woman *not* to trust him. And he did not want to be mistrusted now.

"Do you need somebody to go to the store," asked the boy, "maybe to get some milk or something?"

"Don't believe I do," said the woman, "unless you just want sweet milk yourself. I was going to make cocoa out of this canned milk I got here."

"That will be fine," said the boy.

She heated some lima beans and ham she had in the icebox, made the cocoa, and set the table. The woman did not *ask* the boy anything about where he lived, or his folks, or anything else that would embarrass him. Instead, as they ate, she told him about her job in a hotel beauty shop that stayed open late, what the work was like, and how all kinds of women came in and out, blondes, redheads, and Spanish. Then she cut him a half of her ten-cent cake.

"Eat some more, son," she said.

When they were finished eating, she got up and said, "Now here, take this ten dollars and buy yourself some blue suede shoes. And next time, do not make the mistake of latching onto *my* pocketbook *nor nobody else's*—because shoes got by devilish ways will burn your feet. I got to get my rest now. But from here on in, son, I hope you will behave yourself."

She led him down the hall to the front door and opened it. "Good night! Behave yourself, boy!" she said, looking out into the street as he went down the steps.

The boy wanted to say something other than, "Thank you, m'am," to Mrs. Luella Bates Washington Jones, but although his lips moved, he couldn't even say that as he turned at the foot of the barren stoop and looked up at the large woman in the door. Then she shut the door.

Last Whipping

When I went by his house one Sunday morning to pick up my Kodak that he had borrowed, Simple was standing in the middle of the floor in his shirttail imitating a minister winding up his Sunday morning sermon, gestures and all.

He intoned, " 'Well, I looked and I saw a great beast! And that great beast had its jaws open ready to clamp down on my mortal soul. But I knowed if it was to clamp, ah, my soul would escape and go to glory. Amen! So I was not afraid. My body was afraid, a-a-ah, but my soul was not afraid. My soul said whatsoever you may do to my behind, a-a-ah, beast, you *cannot* harm my soul. Amen! No, Christians! That beast *cannot* tear your immortal soul.

That devil in the form of a crocodile, the form of a alligator with
a leather hide that slippeth and slideth through the bayous swamp
—that alligator *cannot* tear your soul!' "

"You really give a good imitation of a preacher," I said. "But
come on and get dressed and let's go, since you say you left my
Kodak at Joyce's. I didn't stop by here to hear you preach."

"I am saying that to say this," said Simple, "because that is the
place in the sermon where my old Aunt Lucy jumped up shouting
and leapt clean across the pulpit rail and started to preaching
herself, right along with the minister.

"She hollered, 'No-ooo-oo-o! Hallelujah, no! It cannot tear your
soul. Sometimes the devil comes in human form,' yelled Aunt
Lucy, 'sometimes it be's born right into your own family. Sometimes the devil be's your own flesh and kin—and he try your
soul—but your soul he cannot tear! Sometimes you be's forced to
tear his hide *before* he tears your soul. Amen!'

"Now, Aunt Lucy were talking about *me* that morning when she
said 'devil.' That is what I started to tell you."

"Talking about you, why?" I asked.

"Because I had been up to some devilment, and she had done
said she was gonna whip me come Monday. Aunt Lucy were so
Christian she did not believe in whipping nobody on a Sunday."

"What had you done?"

"Oh, I had just taken one of her best laying hens and give it to
a girl who didn't even belong to our church; to roast for her
Sunday school picnic, because this old girl said she was aiming to
picnic *me*—except that she didn't have nothing good to eat to put
in her basket. I was trying to jive this old gal, you know—I was
young—so I just took one of Aunt Lucy's hens and give her."

"Why didn't you pick out a pullet that wasn't laying?"

"That hen was the biggest, fattest chicken in the pen—and I
wanted that girl to have plenty to pull out of her basket at that
picnic so folks would make a great big admiration over her and
me."

"How did your Aunt Lucy find out about the hen?"

"Man, you know womenfolks can't keep no secret! That girl
told another girl, the other girl told her cousin, the cousin told her
mama, her mama told Aunt Lucy—and Aunt Lucy woke me up
Sunday morning with a switch in her hand."

"Weren't you too old to be whipped by then?"

"Of course, I was too old to whip—sixteen going on seventeen,
big as a ox. But Aunt Lucy did not figure I was grown yet. And

she took her duty hard—because she always said the last thing my mother told her when she died was to raise me right."

"What did you do when you saw the switch?"

"Oh, I got all mannish, man. I said, 'Aunt Lucy, you ain't gonna whip me no more. I's a man—and you ain't gonna whip me.' "

"Aunt Lucy said, 'Yes, I is, too, Jess. I will whip you until you gets grown enough to know how to act like a man—not just *look* like one. You know you had no business snatching my hen right off her nest and giving it to that low-life hussy what had no better sense than to take it, knowing you ain't got nowhere to get no hen except out of *my* henhouse. Were this not Sunday, I would whale you in a inch of your life before you could get out of that bed.' "

"Aunt Lucy was angry," I commented.

"She was," said Simple. "And big as I was, I was scared. But I was meaning not to let her whip me, even if I had to snatch that sapling out of her hand."

"So what happened on Monday morning?"

"Aunt Lucy waited until I got up, dressed, and washed my face. Then she called me. 'Jess!' I knowed it were whipping time. Just when I was aiming to snatch that switch out of her hand, I seed that Aunt Lucy was crying when she told me to come there. I said 'Aunt Lucy, what you crying for?' "

"She said, 'I am crying 'cause here you is a man, and don't know how to act right yet, and I done did my best to raise you so you would grow up good. I done wore out so many switches on your back, still you tries my soul. But it ain't *my* soul I'm thinking of, son, it's yourn. Jess, I wants you to carry yourself right and 'sociate with peoples what's decent and be a good boy. You understand me? I's getting too old to be using my strength like this. Here!' she hollered, 'bend over and lemme whip you one more time!' "

"Did she whip you?"

"She whipped me—because I bent," said Simple. "When I seen her crying, I would have let her kill me before I raised my hand. When she got through, I said, 'Aunt Lucy, you ain't gonna have to whip me no more. I ain't gonna give you no cause. I do not mind to be beat. But I do not *never* want to see you cry no more—so I am going to do my best to do right from now on and not try your soul. And I am sorry about that hen.' "

"And you know, man, from that day to this, I have tried to behave myself. Aunt Lucy is gone to glory this morning, but if she is looking down, she knows that is true. That was my last whipping. But it wasn't the whipping that taught me what I needed to know. It was because she cried—and cried. When peoples care for you and cry for you, they can straighten out your soul. Ain't that right, boy?"

"Yes," I said, "that's right."

Christmas Song

"Just like a Negro," said Simple, "I have waited till Christmas Eve to finish my shopping."

"You are walking rather fast," I said. "Be careful, don't slip on the ice. The way it's snowing, you can't always see it underneath the snow."

"Why do you reckon they don't clean off the sidewalks in Harlem nice like they do downtown?"

"Why do *you* reckon?" I asked. "But don't tell me! I don't wish to discuss race tonight, certainly not out here in the street, as cold as it is."

"Paddy's is right there in the next block," said Simple, heading steadily that way. "I am going down to 125th Street to get two rattles, one for Carlyle's baby, Third Floor Front, and one for that other cute little old baby downstairs in the Second Floor Rear. Also I aims to get a box of hard candy for my next-door neighbor that ain't got no teeth, poor Miss Amy, so she can suck it. And a green rubber bone for Trixie. Also some kind of game for Joyce to take her godchild from me during the holidays."

"It's eight o'clock already, fellow. If you've got all that to do, you'd better hurry before the stores close."

"I am hurrying. Joyce sent me out to get some sparklers for the tree. Her and her big old fat landlady and some of the other roomers in their house is putting up a Christmas tree down in the living room, and you are invited to come by and help trim it, else watch them trimming. Do you want to go?"

"When?"

"Long about midnight P.M., I'd say. Joyce is taking a nap now. When she wakes up she's promised to make some good old Christmas eggnog—if I promise not to spike it too strong. You might as well dip your cup in our bowl. Meanwhile, let's grab a quick beer here before I get on to the store. Come on inside. Man, I'm excited! I got another present for Joyce."

"What?"

"I'm not going to tell you until after Christmas. It's a surprise. But whilst I am drinking, look at this which I writ yesterday."

XMAS

I forgot to send
A card to Jennie—
But the truth about cousins is
There's too many.

I also forgot
My Uncle Joe,
But I believe I'll let
That old rascal go.

I done bought
Four boxes now.
I can't afford
No more, nohow.

So Merry Xmas,
Everybody!
Cards or no cards,
Here's HOWDY!

"That's for my Christmas card," said Simple. "Come on, let's go."

"Not bad. Even if it will be a little late, be sure you send me one," I said as we went out into the snow.

"Man, you know I can't afford to have no cards printed up. It's just jive. I likes to compose with a pencil sometimes. Truth is, come Christmas, I has feelings right up in my throat that if I was a composer, I would write me a song also, which I would sing myself. It would be a song about that black Wise Man who went to see the Baby in the Manger. I would put into it such another music as you never heard. It would be a baritone song."

"There are many songs about the Three Wise Men," I said. "Why would you single out the black one?"

"Because I am black," said Simple, "so my song would be about the black Wise Man."

"If you could write such a song, what would it say?"

"Just what the Bible says—that he saw a star, he came from the East, and he went with the other Wise Mens to Bethlehem in Judea, and bowed down before the Child in the Manger, and put his presents down there in the straw for that Baby—and it were the greatest Baby in the world, for it were Christ! That is what my song would say."

"You don't speak of the Bible very often," I said, "but when you do, you speak like a man who knew it as a child."

"My Aunt Lucy read the Bible to me all the time when I were knee high to a duck. I never will forget it. So if I wrote a Christmas song, I would write one right out of the Bible. But it would not be so much what words I would put in it as what my music would say—because I would also make up the music myself. Music explains things better than words and everybody in all kind of languages could understand it then. My music would say everything my words couldn't put over, because there wouldn't be many words anyhow.

"The words in my song would just say a black man saw a star and followed it till he came to a stable and put his presents down. But the music would say he also laid his heart down, too—which would be my heart. It would be *my* song I would be making up. But I would make it like as if I was there myself two thousand years ago, and *I* seen the star, and *I* followed it till I come to that Child. And when I riz up from bending over that Baby in the Manger I were strong and not afraid. The end of my song would be, *Be not afraid*. That would be the end of my song."

"It sounds like a good song," I said.

"It would be the kind of song everybody could sing, old folks and young folks. And when they sing it, some folks would laugh. It would be a happy song. Other folks would cry because—well, I don't know," Simple stopped quite still for a moment in the falling snow. "I don't know, but something about that black man and that little small Child—something about them two peoples—folks would cry."

Richard Wright (1908-1960)

The Man Who Was Almost a Man

Richard Wright has been described as the most influential Afro-American novelist who ever lived. Born in Natchez, Mississippi, he dreamed of becoming a writer even while he was undergoing the brutalizing experiences of discrimination in Mississippi and Tennessee. In 1927 he moved to Chicago, where, while working at various jobs, he studied and practiced the craft of fiction. His first book, *Uncle Tom's Children*, a collection of stories about Southern Negroes, appeared in 1938. Although it was well received, Wright feared that he had evoked only an ineffectual pity for black Americans rather than an anger which would incite readers to correct the oppressive conditions. In 1940, he earned international fame with *Native Son*, a shocking indictment of American racism revealed through the story of a black youth who accidentally murders his wealthy employer's daughter. The novel gave new direction to fiction by black Americans. The first novel of social protest by a Negro to be evaluated and praised as a work of art rather than merely as a social document, it encouraged and compelled subsequent black writers to concern themselves with their art rather than merely with their message.

During the remainder of his life, most of it spent in France, Wright published an autobiography—*Black Boy* (1945); an interpretive history of black Americans—*12 Million Black Voices*; nonfiction about Africa, Spain, and racial problems; four novels, and a collection of short stories—*Eight Men*.

In the following story Wright, with characteristic violence, tells of a black American youth who wants to affirm his manhood.

The Man Who Was Almost a Man

Dave struck out across the fields, looking homeward through paling light. Whut's the use talkin wid em niggers in the field? Anyhow, his mother was putting supper on the table. Them niggers can't understan nothing. One of these days he was going to get a gun and practice shooting, then they couldn't talk to him as though he were a little boy. He slowed, looking at the ground. Shucks, Ah ain scareda them even ef they are biggern me! Aw, Ah know whut Ahma do. Ahm going by ol Joe's sto n git that Sears Roebuck catlog n look at them guns. Mebbe Ma will lemme buy one when she gits mah pay from old man Hawkins. Ahma beg her t gimme some money. Ahm ol ernough to hava gun. Ahm seventeen. Almost a man. He strode, feeling his long loose-jointed limbs. Shucks, a man oughta hava little gun aftah he done worked hard all day.

He came in sight of Joe's store. A yellow lantern glowed on the front porch. He mounted steps and went through the screen door, hearing it bang behind him. There was a strong smell of coal oil and mackerel fish. He felt very confident until he saw fat Joe walk in through the rear door, then his courage began to ooze.

"Howdy, Dave! Whutcha want?"

"How yuh, Mistah Joe? Aw, Ah don wanna buy nothing. Ah jus wanted t see ef yuhd lemme look at tha catlog erwhile."

"Sure! You wanna see it here?"

"Nawsuh. Ah wans t take it home wid me. Ah'll bring it back termorrow when Ah come in from the fiels."

"You plannin on buying something?"

"Yessuh."

"Your ma lettin you have your own money now?"

"Shucks. Mistah Joe, Ahm gittin t be a man like anybody else!"

Joe laughed and wiped his greasy white face with a red bandanna.

"Whut you plannin on buyin?"

Dave looked at the floor, scratched his head, scratched his thigh, and smiled. Then he looked up shyly.

"Ah'll tell yuh, Mistah Joe, ef yuh promise yuh won't tell."

"I promise."

"Waal, Ahma buy a gun."

"A gun? Whut you want with a gun?"

"Ah wanna keep it."

"You ain't nothing but a boy. You don't need a gun."

"Aw, lemme have the catlog, Mistah Joe. Ah'll bring it back."

Joe walked through the rear door. Dave was elated. He looked around at barrels of sugar and flour. He heard Joe coming back. He craned his neck to see if he were bringing the book. Yeah, he's got it. Gawddog, he's got it!

"Here, but be sure you bring it back. It's the only one I got."

"Sho, Mistah Joe."

"Say, if you wanna buy a gun, why don't you buy one from me? I gotta gun to sell."

"Will it shoot?"

"Sure it'll shoot."

"Whut kind is it?"

"Oh, it's kinda old . . . a left-hand Wheeler. A pistol. A big one."

"Is it got bullets in it?"

"It's loaded."

"Kin Ah see it?"

"Where's your money?"

"Whut yuh wan fer it?"

"I'll let you have it for two dollars."

"Just two dollahs? Shucks, Ah could buy tha when Ah git mah pay."

"I'll have it here when you want it."

"Awright, suh. Ah be in fer it."

He went through the door, hearing it slam again behind him. Ahma git some money from Ma n buy me a gun! Only two dollahs! He tucked the thick catalogue under his arm and hurried.

"Where yuh been, boy?" His mother held a steaming dish of black-eyed peas.

"Aw, Ma, Ah just stopped down the road t talk wid the boys."

"Yuh know bettah t keep suppah waitin."

He sat down, resting the catalogue on the edge of the table.

"Yuh git up from there and git to the well n wash yosef! Ah ain feedin no hogs in mah house!"

She grabbed his shoulder and pushed him. He stumbled out of the room, then came back to get the catalogue.

"Whut this?"

"Aw, Ma, it's jusa catlog."

"Who yuh git it from?"

"From Joe, down at the sto."

"Waal, thas good. We kin use it in the outhouse."

"Naw, Ma." He grabbed for it. "Gimme ma catlog, Ma."

She held onto it and glared at him.

"Quit hollerin at me! Whut's wrong wid yuh? Yuh crazy?"

"But Ma, please. It ain mine! It's Joe's! He tol me t bring it back t im termorrow."

She gave up the book. He stumbled down the back steps, hugging the thick book under his arm. When he had splashed water on his face and hands, he groped back to the kitchen and fumbled in a corner for the towel. He bumped into a chair; it clattered to the floor. The catalogue sprawled at his feet. When he had dried his eyes he snatched up the book and held it again under his arm. His mother stood watching him.

"Now, ef yuh gonna act a fool over that ol book, Ah'll take it n burn it up."

"Naw, Ma, please."

"Waal, set down n be still!"

He sat down and drew the oil lamp close. He thumbed page after page, unaware of the food his mother set on the table. His father came in. Then his small brother.

"Whutcha got there, Dave?" his father asked.

"Jusa catlog," he answered, not looking up.

"Yeah, here they is!" His eyes glowed at blue-and-black revolvers. He glanced up, feeling sudden guilt. His father was watching him. He eased the book under the table and rested it on his knees. After the blessing was asked, he ate. He scooped up peas and swallowed fat meat without chewing. Buttermilk helped to wash it down. He did not want to mention money before his father. He would do much better by cornering his mother when she was alone. He looked at his father uneasily out of the edge of his eye.

"Boy, how come yuh don quit foolin wid tha book n eat yo suppah?"

"Yessuh."

"How you n ol man Hawkins gitten erlong?"

"Suh?"

"Can't yuh hear? Why don yuh lissen? Ah ast yu how wuz yuh n ol man Hawkins gittin erlong?"

"Oh, swell, Pa. Ah plows mo lan than anybody over there."

"Waal, yuh oughta keep yo mind on whut yuh doin."

"Yessuh."

He poured his plate full of molasses and sopped it up slowly with a chunk of cornbread. When his father and brother had left the kitchen, he still sat and looked again at the guns in the catalogue, longing to muster courage enough to present his case to his mother. Lawd, ef Ah only had tha pretty one! He could almost feel the slickness of the weapon with his fingers. If he had a gun like that he would polish it and keep it shining so it would never rust. N Ah'd keep it loaded, by Gawd!

"Ma?" His voice was hesitant.

"Hunh?"

"Ol man Hawkins give yuh mah money yit?"

"Yeah, but ain no usa yuh thinking bout throwin nona it erway. Ahm keepin tha money sos yuh kin have cloes t go to school this winter."

He rose and went to her side with the open catalogue in his palms. She was washing dishes, her head bent low over a pan. Shyly he raised the book. When he spoke, his voice was husky, faint.

"Ma, Gawd knows Ah wans one of these."

"One of whut?" she asked, not raising her eyes.

"One of these," he said again, not daring even to point. She glanced up at the page, then at him with wide eyes.

"Nigger, is yuh gone plumb crazy?"

"Aw, Ma—"

"Git outta here! Don yuh talk t me bout no gun! Yuh a fool!"

"Ma, Ah kin buy one fer two dollahs."

"Not ef Ah knows it, yuh ain!"

"But yuh promised me one—"

"Ah don care whut Ah promised! Yuh ain nothing but a boy yit!"

"Ma, ef yuh lemme buy one Ah'll *never* ast yuh fer nothing no mo."

"Ah tol yuh t git outta here! Yuh ain gonna toucha penny of tha money fer no gun! Thas how come Ah has Mistah Hawkins t pay yo wages t me, cause Ah knows yuh ain got no sense."

"But, Ma, we needa gun. Pa ain got no gun. We needa gun in the house. Yuh kin never tell whut might happen."

"Now don yuh try to maka fool outta me, boy! Ef we did hava gun, yuh wouldn't have it!"

He laid the catalogue down and slipped his arm around her waist.

"Aw, Ma, Ah done worked hard alla summer n ain ast yuh fer nothing, is Ah, now?"

"Thas whut yuh spose t do!"

"But Ma, Ah wans a gun. Yuh kin lemme have two dollahs outta mah money. Please, Ma. I kin give it to Pa . . . Please, Ma! Ah loves yuh, Ma."

When she spoke her voice came soft and low.

"Whut yu wan wida gun, Dave? Yuh don need no gun. Yuh'll git in trouble. N ef yo pa jus thought Ah let yuh have money t buy a gun he'd hava fit."

"Ah'll hide it, Ma. It ain but two dollahs."

"Lawd, chil, whut's wrong wid yuh?"

"Ain nothin wrong, Ma. Ahm almos a man now. Ah wans a gun."

"Who gonna sell yuh a gun?"

"Ol Joe at the sto."

"N it don cos but two dollahs?"

"Thas all, Ma. Jus two dollahs. Please, Ma."

She was stacking the plates away; her hands moved slowly, reflectively. Dave kept an anxious silence. Finally, she turned to him.

"Ah'll let yuh git tha gun ef yuh promise me one thing."

"Whut's tha, Ma?"

"Yuh bring it straight back t me, yuh hear? It be fer Pa."

"Yessum! Lemme go now, Ma."

She stooped, turned slightly to one side, raised the hem of her dress, rolled down the top of her stocking, and came up with a slender wad of bills.

"Here," she said. "Lawd knows yuh don need no gun. But yer pa does. Yuh bring it right back t me, yuh hear? Ahma put it up. Now ef yuh don, Ahma have yuh pa lick yuh so hard yuh won fergit it."

"Yessum."

He took the money, ran down the steps, and across the yard.

"Dave! Yuuuuuh Daaaaave!"

He heard, but he was not going to stop now. "Naw, Lawd!"

The first movement he made the following morning was to reach under his pillow for the gun. In the gray light of dawn he held it loosely, feeling a sense of power. Could kill a man with a gun like this. Kill anybody, black or white. And if he were holding his gun in his hand, nobody could run over him; they would have to respect him. It was a big gun, with a long barrel and a heavy handle. He raised and lowered it in his hand, marveling at its weight.

He had not come straight home with it as his mother had asked; instead he had stayed out in the fields, holding the weapon in his hand, aiming it now and then at some imaginary foe. But he had not fired it; he had been afraid that his father might hear. Also he was not sure he knew how to fire it.

To avoid surrendering the pistol he had not come into the house until he knew that they were all asleep. When his mother had tiptoed to his bedside late that night and demanded the gun, he had first played possum; then he had told her that the gun was hidden outdoors, that he would bring it to her in the morning. Now he lay turning it slowly in his hands. He broke it, took out the cartridges, felt them, and then put them back.

He slid out of bed, got a long strip of old flannel from a trunk, wrapped the gun in it, and tied it to his naked thigh while it was still loaded. He did not go in to breakfast. Even though it was not yet daylight, he started for Jim Hawkins' plantation. Just as the sun was rising he reached the barns where the mules and plows were kept.

"Hey! That you, Dave?"

He turned. Jim Hawkins stood eying him suspiciously.

"What're yuh going here so early?"

"Ah didn't know Ah wuz gittin up so early, Mistah Hawkins. Ah wuz fixin t hitch up ol Jenny n take her t the fiels."

"Good. Since you're so early, how about plowing that stretch down by the woods?"

"Suits me, Mistah Hawkins."

"O.K. Go to it!"

He hitched Jenny to a plow and started across the fields. Hot dog! This was just what he wanted. If he could get down by the woods, he could shoot his gun and nobody would hear. He walked behind the plow, hearing the traces creaking, feeling the gun tied tight to his thigh.

When he reached the woods, he plowed two whole rows before he decided to take out the gun. Finally, he stopped, looked in all directions, then untied the gun and held it in his hand. He turned to the mule and smiled.

"Know whut this is, Jenny? Naw, yuh wouldn know! Yuhs jusa ol mule! Anyhow, this is a gun, n it kin shoot, by Gawd!"

He held the gun at arm's length. Whut t hell, Ahma shoot this thing! He looked at Jenny again.

"Lissen here, Jenny! When Ah pull this ol trigger, Ah don wan yuh t run n acka fool now!"

Jenny stood with head down, her short ears pricked straight. Dave walked off about twenty feet, held the gun far out from him at arm's length, and turned his head. Hell, he told himself, Ah ain afraid. The gun felt loose in his fingers; he waved it wildly for a moment. Then he shut his eyes and tightened his forefinger. Bloom! A report half deafened him and he thought his right hand was torn from his arm. He heard Jenny whinnying and galloping over the field, and he found himself on his knees, squeezing his fingers hard between his legs. His hand was numb; he jammed it into his mouth, trying to warm it, trying to stop the pain. The gun lay at his feet. He did not quite know what had happened. He stood up and stared at the gun as though it were a living thing. He gritted his teeth and kicked the gun. Yuh almos broke mah arm! He turned to look for Jenny; she was far over the fields, tossing her head and kicking wildly.

"Hol on there, ol mule!"

When he caught up with her she stood trembling, walling her big white eyes at him. The plow was far away; the traces had broken. Then Dave stopped short, looking, not believing. Jenny was bleeding. Her left side was red and wet with blood. He went closer. Lawd, have mercy! Wondah did Ah shoot this mule? He grabbed for Jenny's mane. She flinched, snorted, whirled, tossing her head.

"Hol on now! Hol on."

Then he saw the hole in Jenny's side, right between the ribs. It was round, wet, red. A crimson stream streaked down the front leg, flowing fast. Good Gawd! Ah wuzn't shootin at tha mule. He felt panic. He knew he had to stop that blood, or Jenny would bleed to death. He had never seen so much blood in all his life. He chased the mule for half a mile, trying to catch her. Finally she stopped, breathing hard, stumpy tail half arched. He caught her mane and led her back to where the plow and gun lay. Then he stooped and grabbed handfuls of damp black earth and tried to plug the bullet hole. Jenny shuddered, whinnied, and broke from him.

"Hol on! Hol on now!"

He tried to plug it again, but blood came anyhow. His fingers were hot and sticky. He rubbed dirt into his palms, trying to dry them. Then again he attempted to plug the bullet hole, but Jenny shied away, kicking her heels high. He stood helpless. He had to do something. He ran at Jenny; she dodged him. He watched a red stream of blood flow down Jenny's leg and form a bright pool at her feet.

"Jenny . . . Jenny," he called weakly.

His lips trembled. She's bleeding t death! He looked in the direction of home, wanting to go back, wanting to get help. But he saw the pistol lying in the damp black clay. He had a queer feeling that if he only did something, this would not be; Jenny would not be there bleeding to death.

When he went to her this time, she did not move. She stood with sleepy, dreamy eyes; and when he touched her she gave a low-pitched whinny and knelt to the ground, her front knees slopping in blood.

"Jenny . . . Jenny . . ." he whispered.

For a long time she held her neck erect; then her head sank, slowly. Her ribs swelled with a mighty heave and she went over.

Dave's stomach felt empty, very empty. He picked up the gun and held it gingerly between his thumb and forefinger. He buried it at the foot of a tree. He took a stick and tried to cover the pool of blood with dirt—but what was the use? There was Jenny lying with her mouth open and her eyes walled and glassy. He could not tell Jim Hawkins he had shot his mule. But he had to tell something. Yeah, Ah'll tell em Jenny started gittin wil n fell on the joint of the plow. . . . But that would hardly happen to a mule. He walked across the field slowly, head down.

It was sunset. Two of Jim Hawkins' men were over near the edge of the woods digging a hole in which to bury Jenny. Dave was surrounded by a knot of people, all of whom were looking down at the dead mule.

"I don't see how in the world it happened," said Jim Hawkins for the tenth time.

The crowd parted and Dave's mother, father, and small brother pushed into the center.

"Where Dave?" his mother called.

"There he is," said Jim Hawkins.

His mother grabbed him.

"Whut happened, Dave? Whut yuh done?"

"Nothin."

"C mon, boy, talk," his father said.

Dave took a deep breath and told the story he knew nobody believed.

"Waal," he drawled. "Ah brung ol Jenny down here sos Ah could do mah plowin. Ah plowed bout two rows, just like yuh see." He stopped and pointed at the long rows of upturned earth. "Then somethin musta been wrong wid ol Jenny. She wouldn ack right a-tall. She started snortin n kickin her heels. Ah tried t hol her, but she pulled erway, rearin n goin in. Then when the point of the

plow was stickin up in the air, she swung erroun n twisted herself
back on it . . . She stuck herself n started t bleed. N fo Ah could do
anything, she wuz dead."

"Did you ever hear of anything like that in all your life?" asked
Jim Hawkins.

There were white and black standing in the crowd. They murmured. Dave's mother came close to him and looked hard into his
face. "Tell the truth, Dave," she said.

"Looks like a bullet hole to me," said one man.

"Dave, whut yuh do wid the gun?" his mother asked.

The crowd surged in, looking at him. He jammed his hands into
his pockets, shook his head slowly from left to right, and backed
away. His eyes were wide and painful.

"Did he hava gun?" asked Jim Hawkins.

"By Gawd, Ah tol yuh tha wuz a gun wound," said a man,
slapping his thigh.

His father caught his shoulders and shook him till his teeth
rattled.

"Tell whut happened, yuh rascal! Tell whut . . ."

Dave looked at Jenny's stiff legs and began to cry.

"Whut yuh do wid tha gun?" his mother asked.

"Whut wuz he doin wida gun?" his father asked.

"Come on and tell the truth," said Hawkins. "Ain't nobody
going to hurt you . . ."

His mother crowded close to him.

"Did yuh shoot tha mule, Dave?"

Dave cried, seeing blurred white and black faces.

"Ahh ddinn gggo tt sshooot hher . . . Ah ssswear ffo Gawd Ahh
ddin. . . . Ah wuz a-tryin t sssee ef the old gggun would sshoot—"

"Where yuh git the gun from?" his father asked.

"Ah got it from Joe, at the sto."

"Where yuh git the money?"

"Ma give it t me."

"He kept worryin me, Bob. Ah had t. Ah tol im t bring the gun
right back t me . . . I was fer yuh, the gun."

"But how yuh happen to shoot that mule?" asked Jim Hawkins.

"Ah wuzn shootin at the mule, Mistah Hawkins. The gun
jumped when Ah pulled the trigger . . . N fo Ah knowed anythin
Jenny was there a-bleedin."

Somebody in the crowd laughed. Jim Hawkins walked close to
Dave and looked into his face.

"Well, looks like you have bought you a mule, Dave."

"Ah swear fo Gawd, Ah didn go t kill the mule, Mistah Hawkins!"

"But you killed her!"

All the crowd was laughing now. They stood on tiptoe and poked heads over one another's shoulders.

"Well, boy, looks like yuh done bought a dead mule! Hahaha!"

"Ain tha ershame."

"Hohohohoho."

Dave stood, head down, twisting his feet in the dirt.

"Well, you needn't worry about it, Bob," said Jim Hawkins to Dave's father. "Just let the boy keep on working and pay me two dollars a month."

"Whut yuh wan fer yo mule, Mistah Hawkins?"

Jim Hawkins screwed up his eyes.

"Fifty dollars."

"Whut yuh do wid tha gun?" Dave's father demanded.

Dave said nothing.

"Yuh wan me t take a tree n beat yuh till yuh talk!"

"Nawsuh!"

"Whut yuh do wid it?"

"Ah throwed it erway."

"Where?"

"Ah . . . Ah throwed it in the creek."

"Waal, c mon home. N firs thing in the mawnin git to tha creek n fin tha gun."

"Yessuh."

"Whut yuh pay fer it?"

"Two dollahs."

"Take tha gun n git yo money back n carry it t Mistah Hawkins, yuh hear? N don fergit Ahma lam you black bottom good fer this! Now march yosef on home, suh!"

Dave turned and walked slowly. He heard people laughing. Dave glared, his eyes welling with tears. Hot anger bubbled in him. Then he swallowed and stumbled on.

That night Dave did not sleep. He was glad that he had gotten out of killing the mule so easily, but he was hurt. Something hot seemed to turn over inside him each time he remembered how they had laughed. He tossed on his bed, feeling his hard pillow. N Pa says he's gonna beat me . . . He remembered other beatings, and his back quivered. Naw, naw, Ah sho don wan im t beat me tha way no mo. Dam em all! Nobody ever gave him anything. All he did was work. They treat me like a mule, n then they beat me. He gritted his teeth. N Ma had t tell on me.

Well, if he had to, he would take old man Hawkins that two dollars. But that meant selling the gun. And he wanted to keep that gun. Fifty dollars for a dead mule.

He turned over, thinking how he had fired the gun. He had an itch to fire it again. Ef other men kin shoota gun, by Gawd, Ah kin! He was still, listening. Mebbe they all sleepin now. The house was still. He heard the soft breathing of his brother. Yes, now! He would go down and get that gun and see if he could fire it! He eased out of bed and slipped into overalls.

The moon was bright. He ran almost all the way to the edge of the woods. He stumbled over the ground, looking for the spot where he had buried the gun. Yeah, here it is. Like a hungry dog scratching for a bone, he pawed it up. He puffed his black cheeks and blew dirt from the trigger and barrel. He broke it and found four cartridges unshot. He looked around; the fields were filled with silence and moonlight. He clutched the gun stiff and hard in his fingers. But, as soon as he wanted to pull the trigger, he shut his eyes and turned his head. Naw, Ah can't shoot wid mah eyes closed n mah head turned. With effort he held his eyes open; then he squeezed. *Blooooom!* He was stiff, not breathing. The gun was still in his hands. Dammit, he'd done it! He fired again. *Blooooom!* He smiled. *Blooooom! Blooooom! Click, click.* There! It was empty. If anybody could shoot a gun, he could. He put the gun into his hip pocket and started across the fields.

When he reached the top of a ridge he stood straight and proud in the moonlight, looking at Jim Hawkins' big white house, feeling the gun sagging in his pocket. Lawd, ef Ah had just one mo bullet Ah'd taka shot at tha house. Ah'd like t scare ol man Hawkins jusa little . . . Jusa enough t let im know Dave Saunders is a man.

To his left the road curved, running to the tracks of the Illinois Central. He jerked his head, listening. From far off came a faint *hoooof-hoooof; hoooof-hoooof; hoooof-hoooof.* . . . He stood rigid. Two dollahs a mont. Les see now . . . Tha means it'll take bout two years. Shucks! Ah'll be dam!

He started down the road, toward the tracks. Yeah, here she comes! He stood beside the track and held himself stiffly. Here she comes, erroun the ben . . . C mon, yuh slow poke! C mon! He had his hand on his gun; something quivered in his stomach. Then the train thundered past, the gray and brown box cars rumbling and clinking. He gripped the gun tightly; then he jerked his hand out of his pocket. Ah betcha Bill wouldn't do it! Ah betcha ... The cars slid past, steel grinding upon steel. Ahm ridin yuh ternight, so hep me Gawd! He was hot all over. He hesitated just a moment; then he grabbed, pulled atop of a car, and lay flat. He felt his pocket; the gun was still there. Ahead the long rails were glinting in the moonlight, stretching away, away to somewhere, somewhere where he could be a man ...

Frank Yerby (1916-   )

My Brother Went to College

One of the most popular contemporary novelists, Frank Yerby, a native of Augusta, Georgia, received a B.A. from Paine College in that city and an M.A. in English from Fisk University. After teaching briefly, he moved North to work in factories, which paid more money than he was earning as an instructor in Southern Negro colleges in the early Forties.

In his earliest stories, such as "Health Card," which won an O. Henry Award in 1944, Yerby protested against the discriminatory treatment of black Americans. After failing to sell a novel on the same theme, however, he turned to historical or "costume" romances. The first, *The Foxes of Harrow* (1946), told the story of an Irish immigrant who works his way to riches in nineteenth-century Louisiana. Each year since 1946 Yerby has published a novel. Most have been set in the South; all but one have been historical; and most have been best-sellers. Since the early 1950's he has lived in France and Spain.

Occasionally Yerby has been criticized for writing historical romances about white protagonists rather than telling the stories of contemporary Negroes. His detractors accuse him of refusing to assume a role as critic or interpreter of society. It is significant, however, that all of Yerby's novels are written about outcasts who, by intelligence and courage, prove themselves superior to a society which rejects them because of their alien, inferior, or illegitimate birth. It is also significant that, through his white Southern

protagonists, Yerby has ridiculed the most cherished myths identified with the antebellum South.

"My Brother Went to College" exemplifies his early work. It is
strongly contemporary in its treatment of the theme of a youth
who rebels against but later accepts the values of middle-class
society.

My Brother Went to College

When I was very young, the land was a hunger in me. I wanted
to devour it all: plains, mountains, cities teeming with men. Therefore I left the three rooms above the little shop where my father
cobbled shoes, crawling over the still sleeping form of my brother,
Matt, and tiptoeing past the great brass bed in which my father
snored. As I went by, he turned over and murmured, "Mark"; but
he was still sleeping, so I crept by him very quietly and stole down
the creaking stairs. Mark is my name. I suppose that father was
planning to have two more sons and name them Luke and John,
but mother died before he could accomplish it. Afterwards Matt
and I used to argue over whether father, if he had been blessed
with three more sons, would have called the fifth one, "The Acts,"
Matt holding that he would not, and I that he would. Acts of the
Apostles Johnson. It had a very satisfying sound.

I was ten when I ran away from home. When I came back, I was
twenty. For ten years I wandered upon the face of the earth,
hearing the long, sweet, sad, lost, lonesome cry of the train whis-
tles in the night until the sound was in my blood and part of me. I
wandered through the Delta while the sun soaked into my black
hide, and sat on Scott's Bluff near Baton Rouge and watched the
Mississippi run golden with the mud of half a continent. I grew a
lean belly and a knotty calf, and the black wool on my head
kinked tight as cockle burrs. I drank moonshine in the Georgia
swamp country, and rotgut in the Carolina hills. I worked for
spells until I would wake up in the night to hear the trains crying;
then I was off, pushing the earth backward under my feet. I
listened to the whippoorwill at night, and sang with the mocking-
bird in the morning.

I wasn't worth a damn and I didn't care. I was free. I couldn't
keep a job because of that. Sooner or later, the boss would find out
that I could jump to do his orders and still stay free, that I could

be polite and still be free, that you could kick me and cuss me and I could still stay free, because the freedom was inside me. I had soaked it up from the blazing sun in Texas; I had breathed it in with the cool mountain air in Tennessee; I'd drunk it down with all the tepid, muddy, fish-tasting river water. I'd devoured it along with ten thousand miles of timeless space.

I whored from New Orleans to Memphis, and gambled from Louisville to Miami. I was worthless, useless, a ne'er-do-well, a disgrace to my family and I didn't give a damn. But after a while, as I grew older, the hunger lessened in me, and in its place came the great longing to see again the face of my brother, and to walk down streets where people would call out to me as I passed, knowing me, knowing my name. Besides, I had decided to settle down, get me a good job, maybe in the post office, and take a wife.

It took me four days to get home. I didn't even stop to eat. I swung six freights and a fruit truck, and did twenty miles afoot. Then I was walking down the streets of my city, all the well-loved streets, sniffing the smell of the garbage like bouquets of roses, and laughing all over myself. A woman leaned out of a window and said:

"Where you going, pretty brown?"

"Home!" I laughed. "Home!"

"Come on up and I give you luck sho'. Just a dollar to you. Come on up, pretty brown."

"Hell," I said, "I'm black and I sure ain't pretty, and what you got ain't worth no dollar. Leave me be, sister, I'm going home!"

I went around the last corner very slow, making the pleasure last, and there was the old shop just as I'd left it, only a little more run down maybe. Then my heart stopped beating altogether, because the man hammering away at the thick, mostly cardboard, half soles sure Lord wasn't father, or even the half of him.

I walked to the door and I asked him where Deacon Johnson was, who used to keep this shop, and he looked up at me and said:

"He dead. Mighty near six years now since he was laid to rest."

I sat down weakly on one of the high stools.

"And his son—Matt Johnson?" I asked.

"Oh, he here awright. He Doctor Matt Johnson now. Finished up his schoolin' at Mo'house and taken up medicine at Meharry. Fine man, Doctor Johnson. He my doctor. Other night I was taken with a misery in my——"

"Where he live?" I demanded. "I got to see him."

"Way 'cross town. Over there on Westmoreland Drive. What's the matter, son, are you sick?"

"Naw," I said. "Naw, I ain't sick. I'm ever so much obliged to you, mister."

When I had left town, ten years before, only white people had lived on Westmoreland Drive, and big shots at that; so I wasn't at all sure that the new cobbler wasn't stringing me. But that other part sounded all right—all that about the schooling and being a doctor and all. That was just like Matt. There wasn't but one place for him, and that was at the top. That's the way Matt was.

It took me more than a half-hour to get over to Westmoreland Drive. I had to go past five points and through all the city traffic, and after ten years I wasn't exactly clear as to where it was. But I reached it at last, and stood on the corner looking down the shaded street at all the big brick houses sitting high on their green terraces with the automobile driveways curving up and around them, and I drew in my breath and let it out again in one big whoosh. Then I went up to the first house and rang the bell. A young girl came to the door. She had brown skin and soft black hair that curled down over her shoulders. She was so doggoned pretty that I couldn't get my mouth shut.

"Yes?" she said. "Yes?"

"Doctor Johnson," I said, "Doctor Matthew Johnson—do he live here?"

"No," she said, "he lives four houses down on the other side."

Then she smiled at me. I wanted to stand there and just look at her, but then I saw my old rusty shoes and the worn-out fringes at the bottom of my breeches, so I mumbled, "Thank you Ma'am," and went back down the walk to the street.

I stood in front of my brother's house a long time before I got up the nerve to climb up the inclined walk to the door. It was just about the biggest and the best-looking house on the street. Matt had got somewhere, he had. I pushed on the bell button and held my breath. Then the door popped open and a young woman, prettier'n an angel out of Glory, and so light complexioned that I looked at her three times and still I wasn't sure, stuck her head out and said:

"Good evening?"

"Howdy do," I said; "is Matt home?"

"Yes," she said, and her voice was puzzled. "Who shall I tell him is calling?"

"Just tell him, Mark," I said. "He'll know."

She went back in the house, leaving me standing there like a fool. The sunlight slanted through the shade trees on the walk. Where it hit the leaves, it made a kind of blaze. Then it came on through and touched the side of the house, making it a kind of salmon pink.

I heard Matt's big feet come hammering through the hall, then the door banged open, and there he was big as life and twice as handsome. He had on a dark blue suit that must have cost plenty, and his hair was cut close to his skull so that the kink didn't show so much, and his black face was shaved, steamed and massaged until the skin was like black velvet. He took the pipe out of his mouth and stood there staring at me, his Adam's apple bobbing up and down out of the collar of his silk shirt. Then he grinned and said:

"Mark, you crazy little bastard!"

I put out my horny paw, and he took it and wrung it almost off. I was ashamed of myself because all the time I had been standing there thinking that maybe he wouldn't want to see me now, but I should have known better. Matt wasn't like that at all.

He took me by the arm, rags and all, and drew me inside the house. It was a palace. I had seen houses like that in the movies, but nobody could have made me believe that there was a black man anywhere who owned one. The rugs were so soft and deep that they came up to my ankles, and the combination radio-phonograph filled up half of one wall. Sitting in one of the huge chairs was the light girl, and with her were two fat, copper-brown children with soft brown hair almost the color of their skins curling all over their little heads. I just stood there and I couldn't say a word.

It came to me then that Matt had done what I had tried to do, and that he'd done it the right way. He'd built himself a world, and he was free. I had run away from everything and slept in the open fields, hunting for something, and Matt had stayed at home and fought for the same thing and he had got it. I felt less than two inches high.

"Martha," Matt was saying, his voice full of laughter, "this bum you were telling me about is my little brother, Mark."

"Oh," she said. "Oh—I'm so sorry—I didn't know—"

"It's awright, Ma'am," I said. "You was right. I am a bum. I just wanted to see Matt one more time, and now that I have, I reckon I'll be on my way agin."

"Like hell you will!" Matt roared. "You come in the back and have some supper. I promised paw on his death bed that I'd find you, and now that I have, you aren't getting away. Come on now."

He took me to the kitchen, and began to pull stuff out of a huge electric refrigerator and pile it on the table. There was so much food there that I couldn't eat. For the life of me I couldn't. I barely tasted the cold chicken, and ate a tiny piece of cherry pie. And all the time, Matt sat there and looked at me.

"Why didn't you write?" he growled at me. "Any time in the last four years I could have had you back in school—well, it isn't too late now. You're gonna bone up, do you hear me—college preparatory—we'll skip over high—you're too damned old. You'll take pharmacy along with college, and when you're out we'll open a drug store. And Gawddammit, if you fail, I'll break every bone in your stupid body—running off like that!"

I just sat there like a fool and gulped and said, "Yes, Matt, no, Matt, that's right, Matt, that'll be swell." When I had finished, he took me upstairs to the bathroom and drew a tubful of water hot enough to scald the hide off of me.

"Get in," he said, "and give me those clothes." I did as I was told, and he took them out into the hall. I heard him calling the old woman who was his housekeeper. When she got there, I heard him say:

"Take these rags out back and burn them!"

When I got out of the tub he gave me his robe and slippers, and there on the bed was one of his suits and a white shirt and tie and handkerchief and socks and shoes and silk underwear—silk, mind you!

"Get dressed," he growled. "We're going for a walk."

I put on the things, and they fitted except for being a little too big here and there; then we went back down the stairs. Matt put on his hat and kissed his wife and the children, and then we went out on the street. By that time it was dark and the stars hung just above the street lamps. I tried to talk.

"The kids," I said, "Geez, Matt—"

"They're all right," he said. "Martha's swell, too—"

"I'll say," I said. "Where'd you find her?"

"College. You'd better do as well."

"Not me," I said. "She's too light. I wouldn't feel comfortable. I want me a tall brown with white teeth and wide hips. Fat chance, though."

"You get what you go after," Matt said, "and doggone it, I'm gonna see that you go after it! We go in here."

I looked up and saw that it was a barber shop. All the barbers grinned when Matt came in.

"Howdy, Doc," they said, "back so soon?"

"Tom," Matt said to the oldest barber, "this is my brother, Mark. Get out your clippers and give him a close cut. Take that rosary off his head!"

When they had finished with me, I was somebody else. I looked like Matt. I looked prosperous and well fed. I looked important— and just a little, I began to feel important, too.

"Tomorrow night," Matt said, "there's a dance. You're going with us. I want you to meet some nice girls. And for Christsake watch your grammar."

"That girl," I said, "four houses up the street on the other side. Will she be there?"

"Elizabeth? You catch on fast, don't you? Yes, I imagine so. But you won't get a look-in there—she's doggoned popular, I tell you."

"Ain't no harm in trying," I said.

They were nice to me, but I felt strange. Martha went out of her way to make me feel at home. Little Matt and little Martha crawled all over me and called me Uncle, but still I didn't feel right. The mattresses were too soft. I couldn't sleep. The food was so good and so rich that my stomach refused it. And every doggoned one of them, including Matt, talked English like Yankee white folks so that half the time I was saying, "Huh? Whatcha say?"

They said "Courthouse—courrrthouse"—not Co'thouse, like a body ought to do. They said "sure"—not sho'. And they never said "ain't." They talked like the people in pictures—like radio announcers. I admired their proper talk, but it didn't sound right. Martha—all right, she looked the part, but I couldn't get it through my thick skull that anybody black as Matt and I ought to talk like that.

And that dance! I stood by a pillar and looked at the girls—
they had on evening dresses that trailed the floor, and there were
flowers in their hair. And they were all the colors of the rainbow:
soft, velvety nightshade girls, chocolate-brown girls, coppery-
brown girls, gingerbread-brown girls, lemon-yellow girls, old-ivory
colored girls, just off-white girls, and snowy-skinned octoroons
with blond hair and blue eyes.

"Jesus!" I said. "Jesus! Old Saint Peter done gone to sleep and
left open the gates." But I didn't dance. The couples drifted past
me in stately waltzes. Nobody jitterbugged. If anybody had started to, they'd have been thrown out. I felt stiff. I felt frozen. I felt
like the deuce of spades against a king-high flush. I was a lost ball
in high grass. I was a cue ball smack up behind the eight, and the
side pocket was miles away.

I got to get out, I thought. I got to catch myself a freight and
highball it down the river. I can shuffle in a Beale Street juke
joint, where the girls are wide across the beam and you can count
every knee in the place; where you hang a cigarette out the corner
of your mouth and shove your hat back on your head and tickle
the ivories, while you squint your left eye so the smoke won't blind
you; where your sweet gal dances with you, up against you, till her
thighs scald you and you smell her hairgrease under your nose
along with the body sweat and cheap perfume. But in here I can't
breathe, not here, where they drift along like something you dream
about, and the perfume don't come from the dime store, and the
girls move on the air halfway out on your arm. No, by God!

I started toward the door. When I got there, I saw a black boy
in a zoot suit standing there looking in. I felt a great rush of fellow
feeling for him. I was outside looking in, too, although I was inside
the hall. But when I got close, I saw the white policeman that a
city ordinance required at all Negro dances, no matter how respect-
able they were, standing there breaking matches into little pieces
and flipping them into the broad brim of the boy's Big Apple hat.
And the boy was grinning all over his flat face. I turned around
and went back into the hall.

Then she was coming toward me, smiling. I wanted to run. I
wanted to hide. I wanted to kick a hole in the floor and pull it over
me.

"Hello," she said, "I've been looking all over for you."

"You—you been looking all over for me?"

"Yes—Doctor Matt told me you were here. My, but you've changed! Why you're positively handsome with a haircut."

I pulled out a handkerchief and mopped my brow.

"Well," Elizabeth teased, "aren't you going to dance with me?"

I took her in my arms and we moved off. It was like floating— like flying—like dreaming. And I didn't want to wake up. Matt had me. He'd won. The juke boxes in the river joints died away out of mind into silence. I was lost. I could never go back again and I knew it.

"Oh, my God!" I groaned. "Oh, my God!"

I took Elizabeth home after the dance and went through hell wondering whether or not I should try to kiss her, but in the end I decided against it and watched her running up the stairs laughing all over herself. Then I walked home through the gray dawn on Westmoreland Drive that was like no other dawn I'd ever seen. And I thought about how it was with Matt and Matt's crowd: the men in tuxedoes and tails, the women in evening gowns, all very correct, nobody laughing out loud or dancing with their entire bodies or yelling across the dance floor, or saying ain't, or ever doing anything that wasn't on page one of Emily Post, and I wondered if it really felt good to be like that. And while I was wondering, I pushed open the door to the bathroom and found Matt standing before the mirror shaving with a tiny, gold-plated safety razor, and cussing with quiet violence.

He turned around and saw me, and slowly his eyes lit up.

"You!" he said. "You can do it!"

"Do what?" I said.

He put his hand down in his pocket and came out with a ten dollar bill.

"You go downtown today and buy me an old-fashioned straight razor. I hate these damn little things!"

"All right," I said.

"I've been wanting a straight razor for five years," Matt said, touching his jaw with his fingertips.

"Yeah," I said, thinking about Elizabeth.

"I can't always wait to go to the barber shop," Matt said.

"Five years," I said. "Why didn't you just go and buy one?"

Matt turned and looked at me, one half of his face still covered with lather.

"You know I couldn't do that," he said.

"Why not?"

"You know what they'd think I wanted it for."

I looked at Matt and I began to laugh. I laughed so I lost my breath. When I went out into the hall, leaving him there, staring at me, I was still laughing. But I shouldn't have laughed. Even then I must have known it wasn't funny. Now, when I think about it (after all these years, watching my wife, Elizabeth, serving ice cream sodas over the counter of our drug store with her beautiful hands, remembering that Matt did this too), I realize that it was really sad, one of the saddest things, in fact, that I ever heard of.

Ralph W. Ellison (1914-   )

Mister Toussan

Although he has published only two books, Ralph Ellison is one of America's most respected writers. His novel, *Invisible Man* (1952) won the National Book Award when it was first published. Thirteen years later, a poll of more than two hundred authors, critics, and editors selected it as "the most distinguished work published during the past twenty years."

Born in Oklahoma City, Oklahoma, Ellison studied music for three years at Tuskegee Institute. When his college education was interrupted by the need to earn money, he studied sculpture, worked in a variety of occupations—including those of free-lance photographer and professional jazz musician, and wrote essays and reviews for major periodicals. Since publishing *Invisible Man*, he has lectured and taught at several colleges. In 1964, he published *Shadow and Act*, a collection of essays.

Ralph Ellison's short stories are uncollected and relatively unknown because, written while he was undergoing his apprenticeship as a writer, they appeared in magazines less frequently examined by anthologists. "Mister Toussan" comes from this early period. Although the story lacks the sophisticated style, the symbolism, and the satire now identified with Ellison, there is a charming freshness in the sketch of a black boy's first encounter with black history.

Mister Toussan

Once upon a time
The goose drink wine
Monkey chew tobacco
And he spit white lime.
—Rhyme used as a prologue to Negro slave stories.

"I hope they all gits rotten and the worms git in 'em," the first boy said.

"I hopes a big wind storm comes and blows down all the trees," said the second boy.

"Me too," the first boy said. "And when ole Rogan comes out to see what happened I hope a tree falls on his head and kills him."

"Now jus' look a-yonder at them birds," the second boy said, "they eating all they want and when we asked him to let us git some off the ground he had to come calling us little nigguhs and chasing us home!"

"Doggonit," said the second boy, "I hope them birds got poison in they feet!"

The two small boys, Riley and Buster, sat on the floor of the porch, their bare feet resting upon the cool earth as they stared past the line on the paving where the sun consumed the shade, to a yard directly across the street. The grass in the yard was very green and a house stood against it, neat and white in the morning sun. A double row of trees stood alongside the house, heavy with cherries that showed deep red against the dark green of the leaves and dull dark brown of the branches. They were watching an old man who rocked himself in a chair as he stared back at them across the street.

"Just look at him," said Buster. "Ole Rogan's so scared we gonna git some his ole cherries he ain't even got sense enough to go in outa the sun!"

"Well, them birds is gitting their'n," said Riley.

"They mocking birds."

"I don't care what kinda birds they is, they sho in them trees."

"Yeah, ole Rogan don't see *them*. Man, I tell you white folks ain't got no sense."

They were silent now, watching the darting flight of the birds into the trees. Behind them they could hear the clatter of a sewing machine: Riley's mother was sewing for the white folks. It was quiet and as the woman worked, her voice rose above the whirring machine in song.

"Your mamma sho can sing, man," said Buster.

"She sings in the choir," said Riley, "and she sings all the leads in church."

"Shucks, I know it," said Buster. "You tryin' to brag?"

As they listened they heard the voice rise clear and liquid to float upon the morning air:

> *I got wings, you got wings,*
> *All God's chillun got a-wings*
> *When I git to heaven gonna put on my wings*
> *Gonna shout all ovah God's heaven.*
> *Heab'n, heab'n*
> *Everybody talkin' 'bout heab'n ain't going*
>   *there*
> *Heab'n, heab'n, Ah'm gonna fly all ovah God's*
>   *heab'n. . . .*

She sang as though the words possessed a deep and throbbing meaning for her, and the boys stared blankly at the earth, feeling the somber, mysterious calm of church. The street was quiet and even old Rogan had stopped rocking to listen. Finally the voice trailed off to a hum and became lost in the clatter of the busy machine.

"Wish I could sing like that," said Buster.

Riley was silent, looking down to the end of the porch where the sun had eaten a bright square into the shade, fixing a flitting butterfly in its brilliance.

"What would you do if you had wings?" he said.

"Shucks, I'd outfly an eagle, I wouldn't stop flying till I was a million, billion, trillion, zillion miles away from this ole town."

"Where'd you go, man?"

"Up north, maybe to Chicago."

"Man, if I had wings I wouldn't never settle down."

"Me, neither. Hecks, with wings you could go anywhere, even up to the sun if it wasn't too hot. . . ."

". . . I'd go to New York. . . ."

"Even around the stars. . . ."

"Or Dee-troit, Michigan. . . ."

"Hell, you could git some cheese off the moon and some milk from the Milkyway. . . ."

"Or anywhere else colored is free. . . ."

"I bet I'd loop-the-loop. . . ."

"And parachute. . . ."

"I'd land in Africa and git me some diamonds. . . ."

"Yeah, and them cannibals would eat the hell outa you too," said Riley.

"The heck they would, not fast as I'd fly away. . . ."

"Man, they'd catch you and stick soma them long spears in your behin'!" said Riley.

Buster laughed as Riley shook his head gravely: "Boy, you'd look like a black pin cushion when they got through with you," said Riley.

"Shucks, man, they couldn't catch me, them suckers is too lazy. The geography book says they 'bout the most lazy folks in the whole world," said Buster with disgust, "just black and lazy!"

"Aw naw, they ain't neither," exploded Riley.

"They is too! The geography book says they is!"

"Well, my ole man says they ain't!"

"How come they ain't then?"

" 'Cause my ole man says that over there they got kings and diamonds and gold and ivory, and if they got all them things, all of 'em cain't be lazy," said Riley. "Ain't many colored folks over here got them things."

"Sho ain't, man. The white folks won't let 'em," said Buster.

It was good to think that all the Africans were not lazy. He tried to remember all he had heard of Africa as he watched a purple pigeon sail down into the street and scratch where a horse had passed. Then, as he remembered a story his teacher had told him, he saw a car rolling swiftly up the street and the pigeon stretching its wings and lifting easily into the air, skimming the top of the car in its slow, rocking flight. He watched it rise and disappear where the taut telephone wires cut the sky above the curb. Buster felt good. Riley scratched his initials in the soft earth with his big toe.

"Riley, you know all them African guys ain't really that lazy," he said.

"I know they ain't," said Riley, "I just tole you so."

"Yeah, but my teacher tole me, too. She tole us 'bout one of them African guys named Toussan what she said whipped Napoleon!"

Riley stopped scratching in the earth and looked up, his eyes rolling in disgust:

"Now how come you have to start lying?"

"Thass what she said."

"Boy, you oughta quit telling them things."

"I hope God may kill me."

"She said he was a *African?*"

"Cross my heart, man. . . ."

"Really?"

"Really, man. She said he come from a place named Hayti."

Riley looked hard at Buster and seeing the seriousness of the face felt the excitement of a story rise up within him.

"Buster, I'll bet a fat man you lyin'. What'd that teacher say?"

"Really, man, she said that Toussan and his men got up on one of them African mountains and shot down them peckerwood soldiers fass as they'd try to come up. . . ."

"Why good-God-a-mighty!" yelled Riley.

"Oh boy, they shot 'em down!" chanted Buster.

"Tell me about it, man!"

"And they throwed 'em off the mountain. . . ."

" . . . Goool-leee! . . ."

". . . And Toussan drove 'em cross the sand. . . ."

". . . Yeah! And what was they wearing, Buster? . . ."

"Man, they had on red uniforms and blue hats all trimmed with gold, and they had some swords all shining what they called sweet blades of Damascus. . . ."

"Sweet blades of Damascus! . . ."

". . . They really had 'em," chanted Buster.

"And what kinda guns?"

"Big, black cannon!"

"And where did ole what-you-call-'im run them guys? . . ."

"His name was Toussan."

"Toussan! Just like Tarzan. . . ."

"Not *Taar*-zan, dummy, *Toou*-zan!"

"Toussan! And where'd ole Toussan run 'em?"

"Down to the water, man. . . ."

". . . To the river water. . . ."

". . . Where some great big ole boats was waiting for 'em. . . ."

". . . Go on, Buster!"

"An' Toussan shot into them boats. . . ."

". . . He shot into em. . . ."

". . . Shot into them boats. . . ."

"Jesus!! . . ."

"With his great big cannons. . . ."

". . . Yeah! . . ."

"... Made a-brass. ..."

"... Brass. ..."

"... An' his big black cannon balls started killin' them pecker-woods. ..."

"... Lawd, Lawd. ..."

"... Boy, till them peckerwoods hollowed *Please, Please, Mister Toussan, we'll be good!*"

"An' what'd Toussan tell em, Buster?"

"Boy, he said in his big deep voice, *I oughta drown all a-you bastards.*"

"An' what'd the peckerwoods say?"

"They said, Please, Please, *Please, Mister Toussan.* ..."

"... We'll be good," broke in Riley.

"Thass right, man," said Buster excitedly. He clapped his hands and kicked his heels against the earth, his black face glowing in a burst of rhythmic joy.

"Boy!"

"And what'd ole Toussan say then?"

"He said in his big deep voice: *You all peckerwoods better be good, 'cause this is sweet Papa Toussan talking and my nigguhs is crazy 'bout white meat!*"

"Ho, ho, ho!" Riley bent double with laughter. The rhythm still throbbed within him and he wanted the story to go on and on. ...

"Buster, you know didn't no teacher tell you that lie," he said.

"Yes she did, man."

"She said there was really a guy like that what called hisself Sweet Papa Toussan?"

Riley's voice was unbelieving and there was a wistful expression in his eyes which Buster could not understand. Finally he dropped his head and grinned.

"Well," he said, "I bet thass what ole Toussan said. You know how grown folks is, they cain't tell a story right, 'cepting real old folks like grandma."

"They sho cain't," said Riley. "They don't know how to put the right stuff to it."

Riley stood, his legs spread wide and stuck his thumbs in the top of his trousers, swaggering sinisterly.

"Come on, watch me do it now, Buster. Now I bet ole Toussan looked down at them white folks standing just about like this and said in a soft easy voice: Ain't I done begged you white folks to quit messin' with me? ..."

"Thass right, quit messing with 'im," chanted Buster.

"But naw, you-all all had to come on anyway. . . ."

". . . Jus' 'cause they was black. . . ."

"Thass right," said Riley. "Then ole Toussan felt so damn bad and mad the tears come a-trickling down. . . ."

". . . He was really mad."

"And then, man, he said in his big bass voice: Goddamn you white folks, how come you-all cain't let us colored alone?"

". . . An' he was crying. . . ."

". . . An' Toussan tole them peckerwoods: I been beggin' you-all to quit bothering us. . . ."

". . . Beggin' on his bended knees! . . ."

"Then, man, Toussan got real mad and snatched off his hat and started stompin' up and down on it and the tears was tricklin' down and he said: You-all come tellin' me about Napoleon. . . ."

"They was tryin' to scare him, man. . . ."

"Said: I don't give a damn about Napoleon. . . ."

". . . Wasn't studyin' 'bout him. . . ."

". . . Toussan said: Napoleon ain't nothing but a man! Then Toussan pulled back his shining sword like this, and twirled it at them peckerwoods' throats so hard it z-z-z-zinged in the air!"

"Now keep on, finish it, man," said Buster. "What'd Toussan do then?"

"Then you know what he did, he said: I oughta beat the hell outa you peckerwoods!"

"Thass right, and he did it too," said Buster. He jumped to his feet and fenced violently with five desperate imaginary soldiers, running each through with his imaginary sword. Buster watched him from the porch, grinning.

"Toussan musta scared them white folks almost to death!"

"Yeah, thass 'bout the way it was," said Buster. The rhythm was dying now and he sat back upon the porch, breathing tiredly.

"It sho is a good story," said Riley.

"Hecks, man, all the stories my teacher tells us is good. She's a good ole teacher—but you know one thing?"

"Naw; what?"

"Ain't none of them stories in the books! Wonder why?"

"Hell, you know why, Ole Toussan was too hard on them white folks, thass why."

"Oh, he was a hard man!"

"He was mean. . . ."

"But a good mean!"

"Toussan was clean. . . ."

". . . He was a good, clean mean," said Riley.

"Aw, man, he was sooo-preme," said Buster.

"Riiiley!!"

The boys stopped short in their word play, their mouths wide.

"Riley, I say!" It was Riley's mother's voice.

"Ma'am?"

"She musta heard us cussin'," whispered Buster.

"Shut up, man. . . . What you want, Ma?"

"I says I wants you-all to go round in the backyard and play, you keeping up too much fuss out there. White folks says we tear up a neighborhood when we move in it and you-all out there jus' provin' them out true. Now git on round in the back."

"Aw, ma, we was jus' playing, ma. . . ."

"Boy, I said for you-all to go on."

"But, ma . . ."

"You hear me, boy!"

"Yessum, we going," said Riley. "Come on, Buster."

Buster followed slowly behind, feeling the dew upon his feet as he walked upon the shaded grass.

"What else did he do, man?" Buster said.

"Huh? Rogan?"

"Hecks, naw! I'm talkin' 'bout Toussan."

"Doggone if I know, man—but I'm gonna ask that teacher."

"He was a fightin' son-of-a-gun, wasn't he, man?"

"He didn't stand for no foolishness," said Riley reservedly. He thought of other things now, and as he moved along he slid his feet easily over the short-cut grass, dancing as he chanted:

> *Iron is iron,*
> *And tin is tin,*
> *And that's the way*
> *The story. . . .*

"Aw come on man," interrupted Buster. "Let's go play in the alley. . . ."

> *And that's the way. . . .*

"Maybe we can slip around and git some cherries," Buster went on.

> *. . . the story ends*, chanted Riley.

James Baldwin (1924-   )

The Man Child

The best known Afro-American author of this generation, James Baldwin is recognized as a talented writer of fiction and as one of the most distinguished essayists of our time. For many readers his chief merit, demonstrated more effectively in his essays than in his fiction, is his ability to articulate persuasively what it means to be a Negro.

Born and reared in Harlem, Baldwin became a minister when he was fourteen. But, dissatisfied, he left the church to search for his identity, first in America and later in France, where he has lived since 1948. He first aroused critical attention with *Go Tell It on the Mountain* (1953), a semi-autobiographical novel about a youth's religious awakening. Since then he has published three novels, two plays, three collections of essays, and one collection of short stories. His best-known works are *Another Country* (1962), a novel focused on homosexuality and interracial conflicts; *The Fire Next Time* (1963), a long essay explaining the need for black Americans to pity rather than hate their white countrymen; and *Blues for Mr. Charlie* (1964), a dramatization of interracial conflict in the South.

In "The Man Child," Baldwin looks through a white child's eyes at the violent admixtures of love and hate in the world of white adults.

The Man Child

As the sun began preparing for her exit, and he sensed the waiting night, Eric, blond and eight years old and dirty and tired, started homeward across the fields. Eric lived with his father, who was a farmer and the son of a farmer, and his mother, who had been captured by his father on some far-off, unblessed, unbelievable night, who had never since burst her chains. She did not know that she was chained anymore than she knew that she lived in terror of the night. One child was in the churchyard, it would have been Eric's little sister and her name would have been Sophie: for a long time, then, his mother had been very sick and pale. It was said that she would never, really, be better, that she would never again be as she had been. Then, not long ago, there had begun to be a pounding in his mother's belly, Eric had sometimes been able to hear it when he lay against her breast. His father had been pleased. *I did that,* said his father, big, laughing, dreadful, and red, and Eric knew how it was done, he had seen the horses and the blind and dreadful bulls. But then, again, his mother had been sick, she had had to be sent away, and when she came back the pounding was not there anymore, nothing was there anymore. His father laughed less, something in his mother's face seemed to have gone to sleep forever.

Eric hurried, for the sun was almost gone and he was afraid the night would catch him in the fields. And his mother would be angry. She did not really like him to go wandering off by himself. She would have forbidden it completely and kept Eric under her eye all day but in this she was overruled: Eric's father liked to think of Eric as being curious about the world and as being daring enough to explore it, with his own eyes, by himself.

His father would not be at home. He would be gone with his friend, Jamie, who was also a farmer and the son of a farmer, down to the tavern. This tavern was called the Rafters. They went each night, as his father said, imitating an Englishman he had known during a war, *to destruct the Rafters, sir.* They had been destructing The Rafters long before Eric had kicked in his mother's belly, for Eric's father and Jamie had grown up together, gone to war together, and survived together—never, apparently, while life ran, were they to be divided. They worked in the fields all day together, the fields which belonged to Eric's father. Jamie had been forced to sell his farm and it was Eric's father who had bought it.

Jamie had a brown and yellow dog. This dog was almost always with him; whenever Eric thought of Jamie he thought also of the dog. They had always been there, they had always been together: in exactly the same way, for Eric, that his mother and father had always been together, in exactly the same way that the earth and the trees and the sky were together. Jamie and his dog walked the country roads together, Jamie walking slowly in the way of country people, seeming to see nothing, heads lightly bent, feet striking surely and heavily on the earth, never stumbling. He walked as though he were going to walk to the other end of the world and knew it was a long way but knew that he would be there by morning. Sometimes he talked to his dog, head bent a little more than usual and turned to one side, a slight smile playing about the edges of his granite lips; and the dog's head snapped up, perhaps he leapt upon his master, who cuffed him down lightly, with one hand. More often he was silent. His head was carried in a cloud of blue smoke from his pipe. Through this cloud, like a ship on a foggy day, loomed his dry and steady face. Set far back, at an unapproachable angle, were those eyes of his, smoky and thoughtful, eyes which seemed always to be considering the horizon. He had the kind of eyes which no one had ever looked into—except Eric, only once. Jamie had been walking these roads and across these fields, whistling for his dog in the evenings as he turned away from Eric's house, for years, in silence. He had been married once, but his wife had run away. Now he lived alone in a wooden house and Eric's mother kept his clothes clean and Jamie always ate at Eric's house.

Eric had looked into Jamie's eyes on Jamie's birthday. They had had a party for him. Eric's mother had baked a cake and filled the house with flowers. The doors and windows of the great kitchen all stood open on the yard and the kitchen table was placed outside. The ground was not muddy as it was in winter, but hard, dry, and light brown. The flowers his mother so loved and so labored for flamed in their narrow borders against the stone wall of the farmhouse; and green vines covered the grey stone wall at the far end of the yard. Beyond this wall were the fields and barns, and Eric could see, quite far away, the cows nearly motionless in the bright green pasture. It was a bright, hot, silent day, the sun did not seem to be moving at all.

This was before his mother had had to be sent away. Her belly had been beginning to grow big, she had been dressed in blue, and had seemed—that day, to Eric—younger than she was ever to seem again.

Though it was still early when they were called to table, Eric's
father and Jamie were already tipsy and came across the fields,
shoulders touching, laughing, and telling each other stories. To
express disapproval and also, perhaps, because she had heard their
stories before and was bored, Eric's mother was quite abrupt with
them, barely saying, "Happy Birthday, Jamie" before she made
them sit down. In the nearby village church bells rang as they
began to eat.

It was perhaps because it was Jamie's birthday that Eric was
held by something in Jamie's face. Jamie, of course, was very old.
He was thirty-four today, even older than Eric's father, who was
only thirty-two. Eric wondered how it felt to have so many years
and was suddenly, secretly glad that he was only eight. For today,
Jamie *looked* old. It was perhaps the one additional year which
had done it, this day, before their very eyes—a metamorphosis
which made Eric rather shrink at the prospect of becoming nine.
The skin of Jamie's face, which had never before seemed so,
seemed wet today, and that rocky mouth of his was loose; loose
was the word for everything about him, the way his arms and
shoulders hung, the way he sprawled at the table, rocking slightly
back and forth. It was not that he was drunk. Eric had seen him
much drunker. Drunk, he became rigid, as though he imagined
himself in the army again. No. He was old. It had come upon him
all at once, today, on his birthday. He sat there, his hair in his
eyes, eating, drinking, laughing now and again, and in a very
strange way, and teasing the dog at his feet so that it sleepily
growled and snapped all through the birthday dinner.

"Stop that," said Eric's father.

"Stop what?" asked Jamie.

"Let that stinking useless dog alone. Let him be quiet."

"Leave the beast alone," said Eric's mother—very wearily,
sounding as she often sounded when talking to Eric.

"Well, now," said Jamie, grinning, and looking first at Eric's
father and then at Eric's mother, "it *is* my beast. And a man's got
a right to do as he likes with whatever's his."

"That dog's got a right to bite you, too," said Eric's mother,
shortly.

"This dog's not going to bite me," said Jamie, "he knows I'll
shoot him if he does."

"That dog knows you're not going to shoot him," said Eric's
father. "Then you *would* be all alone."

"All alone," said Jamie, and looked around the table. "All
alone." He lowered his eyes to his plate. Eric's father watched

him. He said, "It's pretty serious to be all alone at *your* age." He smiled. "If I was you, I'd start thinking about it."

"I'm thinking about it," said Jamie. He began to grow red.

"No, you're not," said Eric's father, "you're dreaming about it."

"Well, goddammit," said Jamie, even redder now, "it isn't as though I haven't tried!"

"Ah," said Eric's father, "that was a *real* dream, that was. I used to pick *that* up on the streets of town every Saturday night."

"Yes," said Jamie, "I bet you did."

"I didn't think she was as bad as all that," said Eric's mother, quietly. "*I* liked her. I was surprised when she ran away."

"Jamie didn't know how to keep her," said Eric's father. He looked at Eric and chanted: "*Jamie, Jamie, pumkin-eater, had a wife and couldn't keep her!*" At this, Jamie at last looked up, into the eyes of Eric's father. Eric laughed again, more shrilly, out of fear. Jamie said:

"Ah, yes, you can talk, you can."

"It's not my fault," said Eric's father, "if you're getting old— and haven't got anybody to bring you your slippers when night comes—and no pitter-patter of little feet—"

"Oh, leave Jamie alone," said Eric's mother, "he's *not* old, leave him alone."

Jamie laughed a peculiar, high, clicking laugh which Eric had never heard before, which he did not like, which made him want to look away and, at the same time, want to stare. "Hell, no," said Jamie, "I'm not old. I can still do all the things we used to do." He put his elbows on the table, grinning. "I haven't ever told you, have I, about the things we used to do?"

"No, you haven't," said Eric's mother, "and I certainly don't want to hear about them now."

"He wouldn't tell you anyway," said Eric's father, "he knows what I'd do to him if he did."

"Oh, sure, sure," said Jamie, and laughed again. He picked up a bone from his plate. "Here," he said to Eric, "why don't you feed my poor mistreated dog?"

Eric took the bone and stood up, whistling for the dog; who moved away from his master and took the bone between his teeth. Jamie watched with a smile and opened the bottle of whiskey and poured himself a drink. Eric sat on the ground beside the dog, beginning to be sleepy in the bright, bright sun.

"Little Eric's getting big," he heard his father say.

"Yes," said Jamie, "they grow fast. It won't be long now."

"Won't be long *what?*" he heard his father ask.

"Why, before he starts skirt-chasing like his Daddy used to do," said Jamie. There was a mild laughter at the table in which his mother did not join; he heard instead, or thought he heard, the familiar, slight, exasperated intake of her breath. No one seemed to care whether he came back to the table or not. He lay on his back, staring up at the sky, wondering—wondering what he would feel like when he was old—and fell asleep.

When he awoke his head was in his mother's lap, for she was sitting on the ground. Jamie and his father were still sitting at the table; he knew this from their voices, for he did not open his eyes. He did not want to move or speak. He wanted to remain where he was, protected by his mother, while the bright day rolled on. Then he wondered about the uncut birthday cake. But he was sure, from the sound of Jamie's voice, which was thicker now, that they had not cut it yet; or if they had, they had certainly saved a piece for him.

"—ate himself just as full as he could and then fell asleep in the sun like a little animal," Jamie was saying, and the two men laughed. His father—though he scarcely ever got as drunk as Jamie did, and had often carried Jamie home from The Rafters—was a little drunk, too.

Eric felt his mother's hand on his hair. By opening his eyes very slightly he would see, over the curve of his mother's thigh, as through a veil, a green slope far away and beyond it the everlasting, motionless sky.

"—she was a no-good *bitch*," said Jamie.

"She was beautiful," said his mother, just above him.

Again, they were talking about Jamie's wife.

"Beauty!" said Jamie, furious. "Beauty doesn't keep a house clean. Beauty doesn't keep a bed warm, neither."

Eric's father laughed. "You were so—poetical—in those days, Jamie," he said. "Nobody thought you cared much about things like that. I guess she thought you didn't care, neither."

"I cared," said Jamie, briefly.

"In fact," Eric's father continued, "I *know* she thought you didn't care."

"*How* do you know?" asked Jamie.

"She told me," Eric's father said.

"What do you mean," asked Jamie, "what do you mean, she told you?"

"I mean just that. She told me."

Jamie was silent.

"In those days," Eric's father continued after a moment, "all you did was walk around the woods by yourself in the daytime and sit around The Rafters in the evenings with me."

"You two were always together then," said Eric's mother.

"Well," said Jamie, harshly, "at least that hasn't changed."

"Now, you know," said Eric's father, gently, "it's not the same. Now I got a wife and kid—and another one coming—"

Eric's mother stroked his hair more gently, yet with something in her touch more urgent, too, and he knew that she was thinking of the child who lay in the churchyard, who would have been his sister.

"Yes," said Jamie, "you really got it all fixed up, you did. You got it all—the wife, the kid, the house, and all the land."

"I didn't steal your farm from you. It wasn't my fault you lost it. I gave you a better price for it than anybody else would have done."

"I'm not blaming you. I know all the things I have to thank you for."

There was a short pause, broken, hesitantly, by Eric's mother. "What I don't understand," she said, "is why, when you went away to the city, you didn't *stay* away. You didn't really have anything to keep you here."

There was the sound of a drink being poured. Then, "No. I didn't have nothing—*really*—to keep me here. Just all the things I ever knew—all the things—*all* the things—I ever cared about."

"A man's not supposed to sit around and mope," said Eric's father, wrathfully, "for things that are over and dead and finished, things that can't *ever* begin again, that can't ever be the same again. That's what I mean when I say you're a dreamer—and if you hadn't kept on dreaming so long, you might not be alone now."

"Ah, well," said Jamie, mildly, and with a curious rush of affection in his voice, "I know you're the giant-killer, the hunter, the lover—the real old Adam, that's you. I know you're going to cover the earth. I know the world depends on men like you."

"And you're damn right," said Eric's father, after an uneasy moment.

Around Eric's head there was a buzzing, a bee, perhaps, a blue-fly, or a wasp. He hoped that his mother would see it and brush it away, but she did not move her hand. And he looked out again, through the veil of his eyelashes, at the slope and the sky, and then saw that the sun had moved and that it would not be long now before she would be going.

"—just like you already," Jamie said.

"You think my little one's like me?" Eric knew that his father was smiling—he could almost feel his father's hands.

"Looks like you, walks like you, talks like you," said Jamie.

"*And* stubborn like you," said Eric's mother.

"Ah, yes," said Jamie, and sighed. "You married the stubbornest, most determined—most selfish—man I know."

"I didn't know you felt that way," said Eric's father. He was still smiling.

"I'd have warned you about him," Jamie added, laughing, "if there'd been time."

"Everyone who knows you feels that way," said Eric's mother, and Eric felt a sudden brief tightening of the muscle in her thigh.

"Oh, *you*," said Eric's father, "I know *you* feel that way, women like to feel that way, it makes them feel important. But," and he changed to the teasing tone he took so persistently with Jamie today, "I didn't know my fine friend, Jamie, here—"

It was odd how unwilling he was to open his eyes. Yet, he felt the sun on him and knew that he wanted to rise from where he was before the sun went down. He did not understand what they were talking about this afternoon, these grown-ups he had known all his life; by keeping his eyes closed he kept their conversation far from him. And his mother's hand lay on his head like a blessing, like protection. And the buzzing had ceased, the bee, the blue-fly, or the wasp seemed to have flown away.

"—if it's a boy this time," his father said, "we'll name it after you."

"That's touching," said Jamie, "but that really won't do me—or the kid—a hell of a lot of good."

"Jamie can get married and have kids of his own any time he decides to," said Eric's mother.

"No," said his father, after a long pause, "Jamie's thought about it too long."

And, suddenly, he laughed and Eric sat up as his father slapped Jamie on the knee. At the touch, Jamie leaped up, shouting, spilling his drink and overturning his chair, and the dog beside Eric awoke and began to bark. For a moment, before Eric's unbelieving eyes, there was nothing in the yard but noise and flame.

His father rose slowly and stared at Jamie. "What's the matter with you?"

"What's the matter with me!" mimicked Jamie, "what's the matter with me? what the hell do you care what's the matter with me! What the hell have you been riding me for all day like this? What do you want? what do you *want?*"

"I want you to learn to hold your liquor for one thing," said his father, coldly. The two men stared at each other. Jamie's face was red and ugly and tears stood in his eyes. The dog, at his legs, kept up a furious prancing and barking. Jamie bent down and, with one hand, with all his might, slapped his dog, which rolled over, howling, and ran away to hide itself under the shadows of the far grey wall.

Then Jamie stared again at Eric's father, trembling, and pushed his hair back from his eyes.

"You better pull yourself together," Eric's father said. And, to Eric's mother. "Get him some coffee. He'll be all right."

Jamie set his glass on the table and picked up the overturned chair. Eric's mother rose and went into the kitchen. Eric remained sitting on the ground, staring at the two men, his father and his father's best friend, who had become so unfamiliar. His father, with something in his face which Eric had never before seen there, a tenderness, a sorrow—or perhaps it was, after all, the look he sometimes wore when approaching a calf he was about to slaughter—looked down at Jamie where he sat, head bent, at the table. "You take things too hard," he said. "You always have. I was only teasing you for your own good."

Jamie did not answer. His father looked over to Eric, and smiled.

"Come on," he said. "You and me are going for a walk."

Eric, passing on the side of the table farthest from Jamie, went to his father and took his hand.

"Pull yourself together," his father said to Jamie. "We're going to cut your birthday cake as soon as me and the little one come back."

Eric and his father passed beyond the grey wall where the dog still whimpered, out into the fields. Eric's father was walking too fast and Eric stumbled on the uneven ground. When they had gone a little distance his father abruptly checked his pace and looked down at Eric, grinning.

"I'm sorry," he said. "I guess I said we were going for a walk, not running to put out a fire."

"What's the matter with Jamie?" Eric asked.

"Oh," said his father, looking westward where the sun was moving, pale orange now, making the sky ring with brass and

copper and gold—which, like a magician, she was presenting only
to demonstrate how variously they could be transformed—"Oh,"
he repeated, "there's nothing wrong with Jamie. He's been drinking a lot," and he grinned down at Eric, "and he's been sitting in
the sun—you know, his hair's not as thick as yours," and he
ruffled Eric's hair, "and I guess birthdays make him nervous.
Hell," he said, "they make me nervous, too."

"Jamie's *very* old," said Eric, "isn't he?"

His father laughed. "Well, butch, he's not exactly ready to fall
into the grave yet—he's going to be around awhile, is Jamie.
Hey," he said, and looked down at Eric again, "you must think
I'm an old man, too."

"Oh," said Eric, quickly, "I know you're not as old as Jamie."

His father laughed again. "Well, thank you, son. That shows
real confidence. I'll try to live up to it."

They walked in silence for awhile and then his father said, not
looking at Eric, speaking to himself, it seemed, or to the air: "No,
Jamie's not so old. He's not as old as he should be."

"How old *should* he be?" asked Eric.

"Why," said his father, "he ought to be his age," and, looking
down at Eric's face, he burst into laughter again.

"Ah," he said, finally, and put his hand on Eric's head again,
very gently, very sadly, "don't you worry now about what you
don't understand. The time is coming when you'll have to worry—
but that time hasn't come yet."

Then they walked till they came to the steep slope which led to
the railroad tracks, down, down, far below them, where a small
train seemed to be passing forever through the countryside, smoke,
like the very definition of idleness, blowing out of the chimney
stack of the toy locomotive. Eric thought, resentfully, that he
scarcely ever saw a train pass when he came here alone. Beyond
the railroad tracks was the river where they sometimes went swim-
ming in the summer. The river was hidden from them now by the
high bank where there were houses and where tall trees grew.

"And this," said his father, "is where your land ends."

"What?" said Eric.

His father squatted on the ground and put one hand on Eric's
shoulder. "You know all the way we walked, from the house?" Eric
nodded. "Well," said his father, "that's your land."

Eric looked back at the long way they had come, feeling his
father watching him.

His father, with a pressure on his shoulder made him turn; he
pointed: "And over there. It belongs to you." He turned him
again. "And that," he said, "that's yours, too."

Eric stared at his father. "Where does it end?" he asked.

His father rose. "I'll show you that another day," he said. "But it's further than you can walk."

They started walking slowly, in the direction of the sun.

"When did it get to be mine?" asked Eric.

"The day you were born," his father said, and looked down at him and smiled.

"My father," he said, after a moment, "had some of this land—and when he died, it was mine. He held on to it for me. And I did my best with the land I had, and I got some more. I'm holding on to it for you."

He looked down to see if Eric was listening. Eric was listening, staring at his father and looking around him at the great countryside.

"When I get to be a real old man," said his father, "even older than old Jamie there—you're going to have to take care of all this. When I die it's going to be yours." He paused and stopped; Eric looked up at him. "When you get to be a big man, like your Papa, you're going to get married and have children. And all this is going to be theirs."

"And when *they* get married?" Eric prompted.

"All this will belong to *their* children," his father said.

"Forever?" cried Eric.

"Forever," said his father.

They turned and started walking toward the house.

"Jamie," Eric asked at last, "how much land has *he* got?"

"Jamie doesn't have any land," his father said.

"Why not?" asked Eric.

"He didn't take care of it," his father said, "and he lost it."

"Jamie doesn't have a wife anymore, either, does he?" Eric asked.

"No," said his father. "He didn't take care of her, either."

"And he doesn't have any little boy," said Eric—very sadly.

"No," said his father. Then he grinned. "But *I* have."

"*Why* doesn't Jamie have a little boy?" asked Eric.

His father shrugged. "Some people do, Eric, some people don't."

"Will I?" asked Eric.

"Will you what?" asked his father.

"Will I get married and have a little boy?"

His father seemed for a moment both amused and checked. He looked down at Eric with a strange, slow smile. "Of course you will," he said at last. "Of course you will." And he held out his arms. "Come," he said, "climb up. I'll ride you on my shoulders home."

So Eric rode on his father's shoulders through the wide green fields which belonged to him, into the yard which held the house which would hear the first cries of his children. His mother and Jamie sat at the table talking quietly in the silver sun. Jamie had washed his face and combed his hair, he seemed calmer, he was smiling.

"Ah," cried Jamie, "the lord, the master of this house arrives! And bears on his shoulders the prince, the son, and heir!" He described a flourish, bowing low in the yard. "My lords! Behold your humble, most properly chastised servant, desirous of your— compassion, your love, and your forgiveness!"

"Frankly," said Eric's father, putting Eric on the ground, "I'm not sure that this is an improvement." He looked at Jamie and frowned and grinned. "Let's cut that cake."

Eric stood with his mother in the kitchen while she lit the candles—thirty-five, one, as they said, to grow on, though Jamie, surely, was far past the growing age—and followed her as she took the cake outside. Jamie took the great, gleaming knife and held it with a smile.

"Happy Birthday!" they cried—only Eric said nothing—and then Eric's mother said, "You have to blow out the candles, Jamie, before you cut the cake."

"It looks so pretty the way it is," Jamie said.

"Go ahead," said Eric's father, and clapped him on the back, "be a man."

Then the dog, once more beside his master, awoke, growling, and this made everybody laugh. Jamie laughed loudest. Then he blew out the candles, all of them at once, and Eric watched him as he cut the cake. Jamie raised his eyes and looked at Eric and it was at this moment, as the suddenly blood-red sun was striking the topmost tips of trees, that Eric had looked into Jamie's eyes. Jamie smiled that strange smile of an old man and Eric moved closer to his mother.

"The first piece for Eric," said Jamie, then, and extended it to him on the silver blade.

That had been near the end of summer, nearly two months ago. Very shortly after the birthday party, his mother had fallen ill and had had to be taken away. Then his father spent more time than ever at The Rafters; he and Jamie came home in the evenings, stumbling drunk. Sometimes, during the time that his mother was away, Jamie did not go home at all, but spent the night at the farm house; and once or twice Eric had awakened in the middle of the night, or near dawn, and heard Jamie's footsteps walking up and down, walking up and down, in the big room downstairs. It had been a strange and dreadful time, a time of waiting, stillness, and silence. His father rarely went into the fields, scarcely raised himself to give orders to his farm hands—it was unnatural, it was frightening, to find him around the house all day, and Jamie was there always, Jamie and his dog. Then one day Eric's father told him that his mother was coming home but that she would not be bringing him a baby brother or sister, not this time, nor in any time to come. He started to say something more, then looked at Jamie who was standing by, and walked out of the house. Jamie followed him slowly, his hands in his pockets and his head bent. From the time of the birthday party, as though he were repenting of that outburst, or as though it had frightened him, Jamie had become more silent than ever.

When his mother came back she seemed to have grown older—old; she seemed to have shrunk within herself, away from them all, even, in a kind of storm of love and helplessness, away from Eric; but, oddly, and most particularly, away from Jamie. It was in nothing she said, nothing she did—or perhaps it was in everything she said and did. She washed and cooked for Jamie as before, took him into account as much as before as a part of the family, made him take second helpings at the table, smiled good night to him as he left the house—it was only that something had gone out of her familiarity. She seemed to do all that she did out of memory and from a great distance. And if something had gone out of her ease, something had come into it, too, a curiously still attention, as though she had been startled by some new aspect of something she had always known. Once or twice at the supper table, Eric caught her regard bent on Jamie, who, obliviously, ate. He could not read her look, but it reminded him of that moment at the birthday party when he had looked into Jamie's eyes. She seemed to be looking at Jamie as though she were wondering why she had not looked at him before; or as though she were discovering, with some surprise, that she had never really liked him but also felt, in her weariness and weakness, that it did not really matter now.

Now, as he entered the yard, he saw her standing in the kitchen doorway, looking out, shielding her eyes against the brilliant setting sun.

"Eric!" she cried, wrathfully, as soon as she saw him. "I've been looking high and low for you for the last hour. You're getting old enough to have some sense of responsibility and I wish you wouldn't worry me so when you know I've not been well."

She made him feel guilty at the same time that he dimly and resentfully felt that justice was not all on her side. She pulled him to her, turning his face up toward hers, roughly, with one hand.

"You're filthy," she said, then. "Go around to the pump and wash your face. And hurry, so I can give you your supper and put you to bed."

And she turned and went into the kitchen, closing the door lightly behind her. He walked around to the other side of the house, to the pump.

On a wooden box next to the pump was a piece of soap and a damp rag. Eric picked up the soap, not thinking of his mother, but thinking of the day gone by, already half asleep: and thought of where he would go tomorrow. He moved the pump handle up and down and the water rushed out and wet his socks and shoes—this would make his mother angry, but he was too tired to care. Nevertheless, automatically, he moved back a little. He held the soap between his hands, his hands beneath the water.

He had been many places, he had walked a long way and seen many things that day. He had gone down to the railroad tracks and walked beside the tracks for awhile, hoping that a train would pass. He kept telling himself that he would give the train one more last chance to pass; and when he had given it a considerable number of last chances, he left the railroad bed and climbed a little and walked through the high, sweet meadows. He walked through a meadow where there were cows and they looked at him dully with their great dull eyes and moo'd among each other about him. A man from the far end of the field saw him and shouted, but Eric could not tell whether it was someone who worked for his father or not and so he turned and ran away, ducking through the wire fence. He passed an apple tree, with apples lying all over the ground—he wondered if the apples belonged to him, if he were still walking on his own land or had gone past it—but he ate an apple anyway and put some in his pockets, watching a lone brown horse in a meadow far below him nibbling at the grass and flicking his tail. Eric pretended that he was his father and was walking through the fields as he had seen his father walk, looking it all over calmly, pleased, knowing that everything he saw belonged to him. And he stopped and pee'd as he had seen his father do, standing wide-legged and heavy in the middle of the fields; he pretended at the same time to be smoking and talking, as he had seen his father do. Then, having watered the ground, he walked on, and all the earth, for that moment, in Eric's eyes, seemed to be celebrating Eric.

Tomorrow he would go away again, somewhere. For soon it would be winter, snow would cover the ground, he would not be able to wander off alone.

He held the soap between his hands, his hands beneath the water; then he heard a low whistle behind him and a rough hand on his head and the soap fell from his hands and slithered between his legs onto the ground.

He turned and faced Jamie, Jamie without his dog.

"Come on, little fellow," Jamie whispered. "We got something in the barn to show you."

"Oh, did the calf come yet?" asked Eric—and was too pleased to wonder why Jamie whispered.

"Your Papa's there," said Jamie. And then: "Yes. Yes, the calf is coming now."

And he took Eric's hand and they crossed the yard, past the closed kitchen door, past the stone wall and across the field, into the barn.

"But *this* isn't where the cows are!" Eric cried. He suddenly looked up at Jamie, who closed the barn door behind them and looked down at Eric with a smile.

"No," said Jamie, "that's right. No cows here." And he leaned against the door as though his strength had left him. Eric saw that his face was wet, he breathed as though he had been running.

"Let's go see the cows," Eric whispered. Then he wondered why he was whispering and was terribly afraid. He stared at Jamie, who stared at him.

"In a minute," Jamie said, and stood up. He had put his hands in his pockets and now he brought them out and Eric stared at his hands and began to move away. He asked, "Where's my Papa?"

"Why," said Jamie, "he's down at The Rafters, I guess. I have to meet him there soon."

"I have to go," said Eric. "I have to eat my supper." He tried to move to the door, but Jamie did not move. "I have to go," he repeated, and, as Jamie moved toward him the tight ball of terror in his bowels, in his throat, swelled and rose, exploded, he opened his mouth to scream but Jamie's fingers closed around his throat. He stared, stared into Jamie's eyes.

"That won't do you any good," said Jamie. And he smiled. Eric struggled for breath, struggled with pain and fright. Jamie relaxed his grip a little and moved one hand and stroked Eric's tangled hair. Slowly, wondrously, his face changed, tears came into his eyes and rolled down his face.

Eric groaned—perhaps because he saw Jamie's tears or because his throat was so swollen and burning, because he could not catch his breath, because he was so frightened—he began to sob in great, unchildish gasps. "Why do you hate my father?"

"I love your father," Jamie said. But he was not listening to Eric. He was far away—as though he were struggling, toiling inwardly up a tall, tall mountain. And Eric struggled blindly, with all the force of his desire to live, to reach him, to stop him before he reached the summit.

"Jamie," Eric whispered, "you can have the land. You can have all the land."

Jamie spoke, but not to Eric: "I don't want the land."

"I'll be your little boy," said Eric. "I'll be your little boy forever and forever and forever—and you can have the land and you can live forever! Jamie!"

Jamie had stopped weeping. He was watching Eric.

"We'll go for a walk tomorrow," Eric said, "and I'll show it to you, all of it—really and truly—if you kill my father I can be your little boy and we can have it all!"

"This land," said Jamie, "will belong to no one."

"Please!" cried Eric, "oh, please! Please!"

He heard his mother singing in the kitchen. Soon she would come out to look for him. The hands left him for a moment. Eric opened his mouth to scream, but the hands then closed around his throat.

Mama. Mama.

The singing was further and further away. The eyes looked into his, there was a question in the eyes, the hands tightened. Then the mouth began to smile. He had never seen such a smile before. He kicked and kicked.

Mama. Mama. Mama. Mama. Mama.

Far away, he heard his mother call him.

Mama.

He saw nothing, he knew that he was in the barn, he heard a terrible breathing near him, he thought he heard the sniffling of beasts, he remembered the sun, the railroad tracks, the cows, the apples, and the ground. He thought of tomorrow—he wanted to go away again somewhere tomorrow. *I'll take you with me,* he wanted to say. He wanted to argue the question, the question he remembered in the eyes—wanted to say, *I'll tell my Papa you're hurting me.* Then terror and agony and darkness overtook him, and his breath went violently out of him. He dropped on his face in the straw in the barn, his yellow head useless on his broken neck.

Night covered the countryside and here and there, like emblems, the lights of houses glowed. A woman's voice called, "Eric! Eric!"

Jamie reached his wooden house and opened his door; whistled, and his dog came bounding out of darkness, leaping up on him; and he cuffed it down lightly, with one hand. Then he closed his door and started down the road, his dog beside him, his hands in his pockets. He stopped to light his pipe. He heard singing from The Rafters, then he saw the lights; soon, the lights and the sound of singing diminished behind him. When Jamie no longer heard the singing, he began to whistle the song that he had heard.

William Melvin Kelley
(1937-   )

The Only Man on Liberty Street

William M. Kelley is judged by many critics to be one of the most promising novelists of the past decade. Born in New York City, educated at Harvard University, he has won the Reed Literary Prize and the Rosenthal Foundation Award of the National Institute of Arts and Letters.

Kelley earned his first national recognition for *A Different Drummer* (1962), a novel describing the events of a memorable moment in history when all of the Negro residents emigrate from an unnamed Southern state. Since then, Kelley has published *Dancers on the Shore* (1964), a collection of short stories; and *Dem*, a second novel.

In his early work Kelley has been most effective when telling his story through a child, as he does in the following tale of miscegenation in the South.

The Only Man on Liberty Street

She was squatting in the front yard, digging with an old brass spoon in the dirt which was an ocean to the islands of short yellow grass. She wore a red and white checkered dress, which hung loosely from her shoulders, and obscured her legs. It was early spring and she was barefoot. Her toes stuck from under the skirt. She could not see the man yet, riding down Liberty Street, his shoulders square, the duster he wore spread back over the horse's rump, a carpetbag tied with a leather strap to his saddle horn and knocking against his leg. She could not see him until he had dismounted and tied his horse to a small, black, iron Negro jockey and unstrapped the bag. She watched now as he opened the wooden gate, came into the yard, and stood, looking down at her, his face stern, almost gray beneath the brim of his wide hat.

She knew him. Her mother called him Mister Herder and had told Jennie that he was Jennie's father. He was one of the men who came riding down Liberty Street in their fine black suits and starched shirts and large, dark ties. Each of these men had a house to go to, into which, in the evening usually, he would disappear. Only women and children lived on Liberty Street. All of them were Negroes. Some of the women were quite dark, but most were coffee-color. They were all very beautiful. Her mother was light. She was tall, had black eyes, and black hair so long she could sit on it.

The man standing over her was the one who came to her house once or twice a week. He was never there in the morning when Jennie got up. He was tall, and thin, and blond. He had a short beard that looked as coarse as the grass beneath her feet. His eyes were blue, like Jennie's. He did not speak English very well. Jennie's mother had told her he came from across the sea and Jennie often wondered if he went there between visits to their house.

"Jennie? Your mother tells me that you ask why I do not stay at night. Is so?"

She looked up at him. "Yes, Mister Herder." The hair under his jaw was darker than the hair on his cheeks.

He nodded. "I stay now. Go bring your mother."

She left the spoon in the dirt, and ran into the house, down the long hall, dark now because she had been sitting in the sun. She found her mother standing over the stove, a great black lid in her left hand, a wooden spoon in her right. There were beads of sweat on her forehead. She wore a full black skirt and a white blouse. Her one waist-length braid hung straight between her shoulder blades. She turned to Jennie's running steps.

"Mama? That man? My father? He in the yard. He brung a carpetbag."

First her mother smiled, then frowned, then looked puzzled. "A carpetbag, darling?"

"Yes, Mama."

She followed her mother through the house, pausing with her at the hall mirror where the woman ran her hand up the back of her neck to smooth stray black hair. Then they went onto the porch, where the man was now seated, surveying the tiny yard and the dark green hedge that enclosed it. The carpetbag rested beside his chair.

Her mother stood with her hands beneath her apron, staring at the bag. "Mister Herder?"

He turned to them. "I will not go back this time. No matter what. Why should I live in that house when I must come here to know what home is?" He nodded sharply as if in answer to a question. "So! I stay. I give her that house. I will send her money, but I stay here."

Her mother stood silently for an instant, then turned to the door. "Dinner'll be on the table in a half hour." She opened the screen door. The spring whined and cracked. "Oh." She let go the door, and picked up the carpetbag. "I'll take this on up." She went inside. As she passed, Jennie could see she was smiling again.

After that, Jennie's mother became a celebrity on Liberty Street. The other women would stop her to ask about the man. "And he staying for good, Josie?"

"Yes."

"You have any trouble yet?"

"Not yet."

"Well, child, you make him put that there house in your name. You don't want to be no Sissie Markham. That white woman come down the same day he died and moved Sissie and her children right into the gutter. You get that house put in your name. You hear?"

"Yes."

"How is it? It different?"

Her mother would look dazed. "Yes, it different. He told me to call him Maynard."

The other women were always very surprised.

At first, Jennie too was surprised. The man was always there in the morning and sometimes even woke her up. Her mother no longer called him Mister Herder, and at odd times, though still quite seldom, said, No. She had never before heard her mother say

No to anything the man ever said. It was not long before Jennie was convinced that he actually was her father. She began to call him Papa.

Daily now a white woman had been driving by their house. Jennie did not know who she was or what she wanted, but playing in the yard, would see the white woman's gray buggy turn the corner and come slowly down the block, pulled by a speckled horse that trudged in the dry dust. A Negro driver sat erect in his black uniform, a whip in his fist. The white woman would peer at the house as if looking for an address or something special. She would look at the curtained windows, looking for someone, and sometimes even at Jennie. The look was not kind or tender, but hard and angry as if she knew something bad about the child.

Then one day the buggy stopped, the Negro pulling gently on the reins. The white woman leaned forward, spoke to the driver and handed him a small pink envelope. He jumped down, opened the gate, and without looking at Jennie, his face dark and shining, advanced on the porch, up the three steps, which knocked hollow beneath his boots, opened the screen door and twisted the polished brass bell key in the center of the open, winter door.

Her mother came drying her hands. The Negro reached out the envelope and her mother took it, looking beyond him for an instant at the buggy and the white woman who returned her look coldly. As the Negro turned, her mother opened the letter, and read it, moving her lips slightly. Then Jennie could see the twinkling at the corners of her eyes. Her mother stood framed in the black square of doorway, tall, fair, the black hair swept to hide her ears, her eyes glistening.

Jennie turned back to the white woman now and saw her lean deeper into her seat. Then she pulled forward. "Do you understand what I will have them do?" She was shouting shrilly and spoke like Jennie's father. "You tell him he has got one wife! You are something different!" She leaned back again, waved her gloved hand and the buggy lurched down the street, gained speed, and jangled out of sight around the corner.

Jennie was on her feet and pounding up the stairs. "Mama?"

"Go play, Jennie. Go on now, *play!*" Still her mother stared straight ahead, as if the buggy and the white woman remained in front of the house. She still held the letter as if to read it. The corners of her eyes were wet. Then she turned and went into the house. The screen door clacked behind her.

At nights now Jennie waited by the gate in the yard for her father to turn the corner, walking. In the beginning she had been waiting too for the one day he would not turn the corner. But each night he came, that day seemed less likely to come. Even so, she was always surprised to see him. When she did, she would wave, timidly, raising her hand only to her shoulder, wiggling only her fingers, as if to wave too wildly would somehow cause the entire picture of his advancing to collapse as only a slight wind would be enough to disarrange a design of feathers.

That night too she waved and saw him raise his hand high over his head, greeting her. She backed away when he reached the gate so he might open it, her head thrown way back, looking up at him.

"Well, my Jennie, what kind of day did you have?"

She only smiled, then remembered the white woman. "A woman come to visit Mama. She come in a buggy and give her a letter too. She made Mama cry."

His smile fled. He sucked his tongue, angry now. "We go see what is wrong. Come." He reached for her hand.

Her mother was in the kitchen. She looked as if she did not really care what she was doing or how, walking from pump to stove, stove to cupboard in a deep trance. The pink envelope was on the table.

She turned to them. Her eyes were red. Several strands of hair stuck to her temples. She cleared her nose and pointed to the letter. "She come today."

Her father let go Jennie's hand, picked up the letter and read it. When he was finished he took it to the stove and dropped it into the flame. There was a puff of smoke before he replaced the lid. He shook his head. "She cannot make me go back, Josephine."

Her mother fell heavily into a wooden chair, beginning to cry again. "But she's white, Maynard."

He raised his eyebrows like a priest or a displeased school teacher. "Your skin is whiter."

"My mother was a slave."

He threw up his hands, making fists. "Your mother did not ask to be a slave!" Then he went to her, crouched on his haunches before her, speaking quietly. "No one can make me go back."

"But she can get them to do what she say." She turned her gaze on Jennie, but looked away quickly. "You wasn't here after the war. But I seen things. I seen things happen to field niggers that . . . I was up in the house; they didn't bother me. My own father, General Dewey Willson, he stood on a platform in the center of town and promised to keep the niggers down. I was close by." She took his face in her hands. "Maynard, maybe you better go back, leastways—"

"I go back—dead! You hear? Dead. These children, these cowardly children in their masks will not move me! I go back dead. That is all. We do not discuss it." And he was gone. Jennie heard him thundering down the hall, knocking against the table near the stairs, going up to the second floor.

Her mother was looking at her now, her eyes even more red than before, her lips trembling, her hands active in her lap. "Jennie?"

"Yes, Mama." She took a step toward her, staring into the woman's eyes.

"Jennie, I want you to promise me something and not forget it."

"Yes, Mama." She was between her mother's knees, felt the woman's hands clutching her shoulders.

"Jennie, you'll be right pretty when you get grown. Did you know that? Promise me you'll go up North. Promise me if I'm not here when you get eighteen, you'll go north and get married. You understand?"

Jennie was not sure she did. She could not picture the North, except that she had heard once it was cold and white things fell from the sky. She could not picture being eighteen and her mother not being there. But she knew her mother wanted her to understand and she lied. "Yes, Mama."

"Repeat what I just said."

She did. Her mother kissed her mouth, the first time ever.

From the kitchen below came their voices. Her father's voice sounded hard, cut short; Jennie knew he had made a decision and was sticking to it. Her mother was pleading, trying to change his mind. It was July the Fourth, the day of the shooting match.

She dressed in her Sunday clothes and coming downstairs, heard her mother: "Maynard, please don't take her." She was frantic now. "I'm begging you. Don't take that child with you today."

"I take her. We do not discuss it. I take her. Those sneaking cowards in their masks . . ." Jennie knew now what they were talking about. Her father had promised to take her to the shooting match. For some reason, her mother feared there would be trouble if Jennie went downtown. She did not know why her mother felt that way, except that it might have something to do with the white woman, who continued to ride by their house each morning, after her father had left for the day. Perhaps her mother did not want to be alone in the house when the white woman drove by in

her gray buggy, even though she had not stopped the buggy since
the day two months ago, when the Negro had given her mother the
pink envelope.

But other strange things had happened after that. In the beginning she and her mother, as always before, had gone downtown to
the market, to shop amid the bright stalls brimming with green
and yellow vegetables and brick-red meats, tended by dark, country Negroes in shabby clothes and large straw hats. It would get
very quiet when they passed, and Jennie would see the Negroes
look away, fear in their eyes, and knots of white men watching,
sometimes giggling. But the white women in fine clothes were the
most frightening; sitting on the verandas or passing in carriages,
some even coming to their windows, they would stare angrily as if
her mother had done something terrible to each one personally, as
if all these white women could be the one who drove by each
morning. Her mother would walk through it all, her back straight,
very like her father's, the bun into which she wove her waist-
length braid on market days, gleaming dark.

In the beginning they had gone to the suddenly quiet market.
But now her mother hardly set foot from the house, and the food
was brought to them in a carton by a crippled Negro boy, who was
coming just as Jennie and her father left the house that morning.

Balancing the carton on his left arm, he removed his ragged hat
and smiled. "Morning, Mister Herder. Good luck at the shooting
match, sir." His left leg was short and he seemed to tilt.

Her father nodded. "Thank you, Felix. I do my best."

"Then you a sure thing, Mister Herder." He replaced his hat
and went on around the house.

Walking, her hand in her father's, Jennie could see some of the
women of Liberty Street peering out at them through their curtains.

Downtown was not the same. Flags and banners draped the
verandas; people wore their best clothes. The Square had been
roped off, a platform set up to one side, and New Marsails Avenue,
which ran into the Square, had been cleared for two blocks. Far
away down the Avenue stood a row of cotton bales onto which had
been pinned oilcloth targets. From where they stood, the bull's-
eyes looked no bigger than red jawbreakers.

Many men slapped her father on the back, and furtively, looked
at her with a kind of clinical interest. But mostly they ignored her.
The celebrity of the day was her father, and unlike her mother,

he was very popular. Everyone felt sure he would win the match; he was the best shot in the state.

After everyone shot, the judge came running down from the targets, waving his arms. "Maynard Herder. Six shots, and you can cover them all with a good gob of spit!" He grabbed her father's elbow and pulled him toward the platform, where an old man with white hair and beard, wearing a gray uniform trimmed with yellow, waited. She followed them to the platform steps, but was afraid to go any farther because now some women had begun to look at her as they had at her mother.

The old man made a short speech, his voice deep, but coarse, grainy-sounding, and gave her father a silver medal in a blue velvet box. Her father turned and smiled at her. She started up the steps toward him, but just then the old man put his hand on her father's shoulder.

People had begun to walk away down the streets leading out of the Square. There was less noise now but she could not hear the first words the old man said to her father.

Her father's face tightened into the same look she had seen the day the letter came, the same as this morning in the kitchen. She went halfway up the stairs, stopped.

The old man went on: "You know I'm no meddler. Everybody knows about Liberty Street. I had a woman down there myself . . . before the war."

"I know that." The words came out of her father's face, though his lips did not move.

The old man nodded. "But, Maynard, what you're doing is different."

"She's your own daughter."

"Maybe that's why . . ." The old man looked down the street, toward the cotton bales and the targets. "But she's a nigger. And now the talking is taking an ugly turn and the folks talking are the ones I can't hold."

Her father spoke in an angry whisper. "You see what I do to that target? You tell those children in their masks I do that to the forehead of any man . . . or woman that comes near her or my house. You tell them."

"Maynard, that wouldn't do any real good *after* they'd done something to her." He stopped, looked at Jennie, and smiled. "That's my only granddaughter, you know." His eyes clicked off her. "You're a man who knows firearms. You're a gunsmith. I know firearms too. Pistols and rifles can do lots of things, but they don't make very good doctors. Nobody's asking you to give her up. Just go back home. That's all. Go back to your wife."

Her father turned away, walking fast, came down the stairs and grabbed her hand. His face was red as blood between the white of his collar and the straw yellow of his hair.

They slowed after a block, paused in a small park with green trees shading several benches and a statue of a stern-faced young man in uniform, carrying pack and rifle. "We will sit."

She squirmed up onto the bench beside him. The warm wind smelled of salt from the Gulf of Mexico. The leaves were a dull, low tambourine. Her father was quiet for a long while.

Jennie watched birds bobbing for worms in the grass near them, then looked at the young, stone soldier. Far off, but from where she viewed it, just over the soldier's hat, a gliding sea gull dived suddenly behind the rooftops. That was when she saw the white man, standing across the street from the park, smiling at her. There were other white men with him, some looking at her, others at the man, all laughing. He waved to her. She smiled at him though he was the kind of man her mother told her always to stay away from. He was dressed as poorly as any Negro. From behind his back, he produced a brown rag doll, looked at her again, then grabbed the doll by its legs, and tore it part way up the middle. Then he jammed his finger into the rip between the doll's legs. The other men laughed uproariously.

Jennie pulled her father's sleeve. "Papa? What he doing?"

"Who?" Her father turned. The man repeated the show and her father bolted to his feet, yelling: "I will kill you! You hear? I will kill you for that!"

The men only snickered and ambled away.

Her father was red again. He had clenched his fists; now his hands were white like the bottoms of fishes. He sighed, shook his head and sat down. "I cannot kill everybody." He shook his head again, then leaned forward to get up. But first he thrust the blue velvet medal box into her hand. It was warm from his hand, wet and prickly. "When you grow up, you go to the North like your mother tells you. And you take this with you. It is yours. Always remember I gave it to you." He stood. "Now you must go home alone. Tell your mother I come later."

That night, Jennie tried to stay awake until he came home, until he was there to kiss her good night, his whiskers scratching her cheek. But all at once there was sun at her window and the sound of carts and wagons grating outside in the dirt street. Her mother was quiet while the two of them ate. After breakfast, Jennie went into the yard to wait for the gray buggy to turn the corner, but for the first morning in many months, the white woman did not jounce by, peering at the house, searching for someone or something special.

Kristin Hunter (1931-   )

Debut

Born in Philadelphia, Pennsylvania, Kristin Hunter is one of the promising novelists of the current decade. She began writing for *The Pittsburgh Courier* several years before she earned a Bachelor of Science in Education from the University of Pennsylvania in 1951. Since then, Mrs. Hunter has had varied experience as a copywriter, an information officer for the city of Philadelphia, and a free lance writer.

Kristin Hunter earned her first significant recognition as a writer when she was awarded a Fund for the Republic prize for her television documentary, "Minority of One," produced by Columbia Broadcasting System in 1956. She has published two novels, *God Bless the Child* (1964) and *The Landlord* (1965).

Rather than following some recent writers who promote "black literature for black people," Mrs. Hunter has interested herself in the interrelationships of white and black Americans and in the emotional crises of urban Negroes. In the following story, she focuses on the daughter of a social-climbing Negro woman, a subject rarely treated by current black authors.

Debut

"Hold *still*, Judy," Mrs. Simmons said around the spray of pins that protruded dangerously from her mouth. She gave the thirtieth

From *Negro Digest,* XVII (June, 1968). Copyright 1968 by Kristin Hunter. Reprinted by permission of Harold Matson Company, Inc.

tug to the tight sash at the waist of the dress. "Now walk over there and turn around slowly."

The dress, Judy's first long one, was white organdy over taffeta, with spaghetti straps that bared her round brown shoulders and a floating skirt and a wide sash that cascaded in a butterfly effect behind. It was a dream, but Judy was sick and tired of the endless fittings she had endured so that she might wear it at the Debutantes' Ball. Her thoughts leaped ahead to the Ball itself . . .

"*Slowly*, I said!" Mrs. Simmons' dark, angular face was always grim, but now it was screwed into an expression resembling a prune. Judy, starting nervously, began to revolve by moving her feet an inch at a time.

Her mother watched her critically. "No, it's still not right. I'll just have to rip out that waistline seam again."

"Oh, Mother!" Judy's impatience slipped out at last. "Nobody's going to notice all those little details."

"They will too. They'll be watching you every minute, hoping to see something wrong. You've got to be the *best*. Can't you get that through your head?" Mrs. Simmons gave a sigh of despair. "You better start noticin' 'all those little details' yourself. I can't do it for you all your life. Now turn around and stand up straight."

"Oh, Mother," Judy said, close to tears from being made to turn and pose while her feet itched to be dancing, "I can't stand it any more!"

"You can't stand it, huh? How do you think *I* feel?" Mrs. Simmons said in her harshest tone.

Judy was immediately ashamed, remembering the weeks her mother had spent at the sewing machine, picking her already tattered fingers with needles and pins, and the great weight of sacrifice that had been borne on Mrs. Simmons' shoulders for the past two years so that Judy might bare hers at the Ball.

"All right, take it off," her mother said. "I'm going to take it up the street to Mrs. Luby and let her help me. It's got to be right or I won't let you leave the house."

"Can't we just leave it the way it is, Mother?" Judy pleaded without hope of success. "I think it's perfect."

"You would," Mrs. Simmons said tartly as she folded the dress and prepared to bear it out of the room. "Sometimes I think I'll never get it through your head. You got to look just right and act just right. That Rose Griffin and those other girls can afford to be careless, maybe, but you can't. You're gonna be the darkest, poorest one there."

Judy shivered in her new lace strapless bra and her old, childish knit snuggies. "You make it sound like a battle I'm going to instead of just a dance."

"It is a battle," her mother said firmly. "It starts tonight and it goes on for the rest of your life. The battle to hold your head up and get someplace and be somebody. We've done all we can for you, your father and I. Now you've got to start fighting some on your own." She gave Judy a slight smile; her voice softened a little. "You'll do all right, don't worry. Try and get some rest this afternoon. Just don't mess up your hair."

"All right, Mother," Judy said listlessly.

She did not really think her father had much to do with anything that happened to her. It was her mother who had ingratiated her way into the Gay Charmers two years ago, taking all sorts of humiliation from the better-dressed, better-off, lighter-skinned women, humbly making and mending their dresses, fixing food for their meetings, addressing more mail and selling more tickets than anyone else. The club had put it off as long as they could, but finally they had to admit Mrs. Simmons to membership because she worked so hard. And that meant, of course, that Judy would be on the list for this year's Ball.

Her father, a quiet carpenter who had given up any other ambitions years ago, did not think much of Negro society or his wife's fierce determination to launch Judy into it. "Just keep clean and be decent," he would say. "That's all anybody has to do."

Her mother always answered, "If that's all *I* did we'd still be on relief," and he would shut up with shame over the years when he had been laid off repeatedly and her days' work and sewing had kept them going. Now he had steady work but she refused to quit, as if she expected it to end at any moment. The intense energy that burned in Mrs. Simmons' large dark eyes had scorched her features into permanent irony. She worked day and night and spent her spare time scheming and planning. Whatever her personal ambitions had been, Judy knew she blamed Mr. Simmons for their failure; now all her schemes revolved around their only child.

Judy went to her mother's window and watched her stride down the street with the dress until she was hidden by the high brick wall that went around two sides of their house. Then she returned to her own room. She did not get dressed because she was afraid of pulling a sweater over her hair—her mother would notice the difference even if it looked all right to Judy—and because she was afraid that doing anything, even getting dressed, might precipitate her into the battle. She drew a stool up to her window and looked out. She had no real view, but she liked her room. The wall hid the crowded tenement houses beyond the alley, and from its cracks and bumps and depressions she could construct any imaginary landscape she chose. It was how she had spent most of the free hours of her dreamy adolescence.

"Hey, can I go?"

It was the voice of an invisible boy in the alley. As another boy chuckled, Judy recognized the familiar ritual; if you said yes, they said, "Can I go with you?" It had been tried on her dozens of times. She always walked past, head in the air, as if she had not heard. Her mother said that was the only thing to do; if they knew she was a lady, they wouldn't dare bother her. But this time a girl's voice, cool and assured, answered.

"If you think your big enough," it said.

It was Lucy Mae Watkins; Judy could picture her standing there in a tight dress with bright, brazen eyes.

"I'm big enough to give you a baby," the boy answered.

Judy would die if a boy ever spoke to her like that, but she knew Lucy Mae could handle it. Lucy Mae could handle all the boys, even if they ganged up on her, because she had been born knowing something other girls had to learn.

"Aw, you ain't big enough to give me a shoe-shine," she told him.

"Come here and I'll show you how big I am," the boy said.

"Yeah, Lucy Mae, what's happenin'?" another, younger boy said. "Come here and tell us."

Lucy Mae laughed. "What I'm puttin' down is too strong for little boys like you."

"Come here a minute, baby," the first boy said. "I got a cigarette for you."

"Aw, I ain't studyin' your cigarettes," Lucy Mae answered. But her voice was closer, directly below Judy. There were the sounds of a scuffle and Lucy Mae's muffled laughter. When she spoke her voice sounded raw and cross. "Come on now, boy. Cut it out and give me the damn cigarette." There was more scuffling, and the sharp crack of a slap, and then Lucy Mae said, "Cut it out, I said. Just for that I'm gonna take 'em all." The clack of high heels rang down the sidewalk with a boy's clumsy shoes in pursuit.

Judy realized that there were three of them down there. "Let her go, Buster," one said. "You can't catch her now."

"Aw, hell, man, she took the whole damn pack," the one called Buster complained.

"That'll learn you!" Lucy Mae's voice mocked from down the street. "Don't mess with nothin' you can't handle."

"Hey, Lucy Mae. Hey, I heard Rudy Grant already gave you a baby," a second boy called out.

"Yeah. Is that true, Lucy Mae?" the youngest one yelled.

There was no answer. She must be a block away by now.

For a moment the hidden boys were silent; then one of them guffawed directly below Judy, and the other two joined in the secret male laughter that was oddly high-pitched and feminine.

"Aw man, I don't know what you all laughin' about," Buster finally grumbled. "That girl took all my cigarettes. You got some, Leroy?"

"Naw," the second boy said.

"Me neither," the third one said.

"What we gonna do? I ain't got but fifteen cent. Hell, man, I want more than a feel for a pack of cigarettes." There was an unpleasant whine in Buster's voice. "Hell, for a pack of cigarettes I want a bitch to come across."

"She will next time, man," the boy called Leroy said.

"She better," Buster said. "You know she better. If she pass by here again, we gonna jump her, you hear?"

"Sure, man," Leroy said. "The three of us can grab her easy."

"Then we can all three of us have some fun. Oh, *yeah*, man," the youngest boy said. He sounded as if he might be about 14.

Leroy said, "We oughta get Roland and J. T. too. For a whole pack of cigarettes she oughta treat all five of us."

"Aw, man, why tell Roland and J. T.?" the youngest voice whined. "They ain't in it. Them was *our* cigarettes."

"They was *my* cigarettes, you mean," Buster said with authority. "You guys better quit it before I decided to cut you out."

"Oh, man, don't do that. We with you, you know that."

"Sure, Buster, we your aces, man."

"All right, that's better." There was a minute of silence.

Then, "What we gonna do with the girl, Buster?" the youngest one wanted to know.

"When she come back we gonna jump the bitch, man. We gonna jump her and grab her. Then we gonna turn her every way but loose." He went on, spinning a crude fantasy that got wilder each time he retold it, until it became so secretive that their voices dropped to a low indistinct murmur punctuated by guffaws. Now and then Judy could distinguish the word "girl" or the other word they used for it; these words always produced the loudest guffaws of all. She shook off her fear with the thought that Lucy Mae was too smart to pass there again today. She had heard them at their dirty talk in the alley before and had always been successful in ignoring it; it had nothing to do with her, the wall protected her from their kind. All the ugliness was on their side of it, and this side was hers to fill with beauty.

She turned on her radio to shut them out completely and began to weave her tapestry to its music. More for practice than anything else, she started by picturing the maps of the places to which she intended to travel, then went on to the faces of her friends. Rose Griffin's sharp, Indian profile appeared on the wall. Her coloring was like an Indian's too and her hair was straight and black and glossy. Judy's hair, naturally none of these things, had been "done" four days ago so that tonight it would be "old" enough to have a gloss as natural-looking as Rose's. But Rose, despite her handsome looks, was silly; her voice broke constantly into high-pitched giggles and she became even sillier and more nervous around boys.

Judy was not sure that she knew how to act around boys either. The sisters kept boys and girls apart at the Catholic high school where her parents sent her to keep her away from low-class kids. But she felt that she knew a secret: tonight, in that dress, with her hair in a sophisticated upsweep, she would be transformed into a poised princess. Tonight all the college boys her mother described so eagerly would rush to dance with her, and then from somewhere *the boy* would appear. She did not know his name; she neither knew nor cared whether he went to college, but she imagined that he would be as dark as she was, and that there would be awe and diffidence in his manner as he bent to kiss her hand . . .

A waltz swelled from the radio; the wall, turning blue in deepening twilight, came alive with whirling figures. Judy rose and began to go through the steps she had rehearsed for so many weeks. She swirled with a practiced smile on her face, holding an imaginary skirt at her side; turned, dipped, and flicked on her bedside lamp without missing a fraction of the beat. Faster and faster she danced with her imaginary partner, to an inner music that was better than the sounds on the radio. She was "coming out," and tonight the world would discover what it had been waiting for all these years.

"Aw, git it, baby." She ignored it as she would ignore the crowds that lined the streets to watch her pass on her way to the Ball.

"Aw, do your number." She waltzed on, safe and secure on her side of the wall.

"Can I come up there and do it with you?"

At this she stopped, paralyzed. Somehow they had come over the wall or around it and into her room.

"Man, I sure like the view from here," the youngest boy said. "How come we never tried this view before?"

She came to life, ran quickly to the lamp and turned it off, but not before Buster said, "Yeah, and the back view is fine, too."

"Aw, she turned off the light," a voice complained.

"Put it on again, baby, we don't mean no harm."

"Let us see you dance some more. I bet you can really do it."

"Yeah, I bet she can shimmy on down."

"You know it, man."

"Come on down here, baby," Buster's voice urged softly dangerously. "I got a cigarette for you."

"Yeah, and he got something else for you, too."

Judy, flattened against her closet door, gradually lost her urge to scream. She realized that she was shivering in her underwear. Taking a deep breath, she opened the closet door and found her robe. She thought of going to the window and yelling down, "You don't have a thing I want. Do you understand?" But she had more important things to do.

Wrapping her hair in protective plastic, she ran a full steaming tub and dumped in half a bottle of her mother's favorite cologne. At first she scrubbed herself furiously, irritating her skin. But finally she stopped, knowing she would never be able to get cleaner than this again. She could not wash away the thing they considered dirty, the thing that made them pronounce "girl" in the same way as the other four-letter words they wrote on the wall in the alley; it was part of her, just as it was part of her mother and Rose Griffin and Lucy Mae. She relaxed then because it was true that the boys in the alley did not have a thing she wanted. She had what they wanted, and the knowledge replaced her shame with a strange, calm feeling of power.

After her bath she splashed on more cologne and spent 40 minutes on her makeup, erasing and retracing her eyebrows six times until she was satisfied. She went to her mother's room then and found the dress, finished and freshly pressed, on its hanger.

When Mrs. Simmons came upstairs to help her daughter she found her sitting on the bench before the vanity mirror as if it were a throne. She looked young and arrogant and beautiful and perfect and cold.

"Why, you're dressed already," Mrs. Simmons said in surprise. While she stared, Judy rose with perfect, icy grace and glided to the center of the room. She stood there motionless as a mannequin.

"I want you to fix the hem, Mother," she directed. "It's still uneven in back."

Her mother went down obediently on her knees, muttering, "It looks all right to me." She put in a couple of pins. "That better?"

"Yes," Judy said with a brief glance at the mirror. "You'll have to sew it on me, Mother. I can't take it off now. I'd ruin my hair."

Mrs. Simmons went to fetch her sewing things, returned, and surveyed her daughter. "You sure did a good job on yourself, I must say," she admitted grudgingly. "Can't find a thing to complain about. You'll look as good as anybody there."

"Of course, Mother," Judy said as Mrs. Simmons knelt and sewed. "I don't know what you were so worried about." Her secret feeling of confidence had returned, stronger than ever, but the evening ahead was no longer the vague girlish fantasy she had pictured on the wall; it had hard, clear outlines leading up to a definite goal. She would be the belle of the Ball because she knew more than Rose Griffin and her silly friends; more than her mother; more, even, than Lucy Mae, because she knew better than to settle for a mere pack of cigarettes.

"There," her mother said, breaking the thread. She got up. "I never expected to get you ready this early. Ernest Lee won't be here for another hour."

"That silly Ernest Lee," Judy said, with a new contempt in her young voice. Until tonight she had been pleased by the thought of going to the dance with Ernest Lee; he was nice, she felt comfortable with him, and he might even be the awe-struck boy of her dream. He was a dark, serious neighborhood boy who could not afford to go to college; Mrs. Simmons had reluctantly selected him to take Judy to the dance because all the Gay Charmers' sons were spoken for. Now, with an undertone of excitement, Judy said, "I'm going to ditch him after the first dance, Mother. You'll see. I'm going to come home with one of the college boys."

"It's very nice, Ernest Lee," she told him an hour later when he handed her the white orchid, "but it's rather small. I'm going to wear it on my wrist, if you don't mind." And then, dazzling him with a smile of sweetest cruelty, she stepped back and waited while he fumbled with the door.

"You know, Edward, I'm not worried about her any more," Mrs. Simmons said to her husband after the children were gone. Her voice became harsh and grating. "Put down that paper and listen to me! Aren't you interested in your child?—That's better," she said as he complied meekly. "I was saying, I do believe she's learned what I've been trying to teach her, after all."

A. Anthologies Including Short Stories

Brawley, Benjamin, ed. *Early Negro American Writers; Selections with Bibliographical and Critical Introduction*. Chapel Hill: University of North Carolina Press, 1935.

Brown, Sterling A., ed. *American Stuff*. New York: Viking, 1937.

_____. Arthur P. Davis, and Ulysses Lee, eds. *The Negro Caravan*. New York: Dryden, 1941.

Calverton, Victor F., ed. *An Anthology of American Negro Literature*. New York: Modern Library, 1929.

Chapman, Abraham, ed. *Black Voices*. New York: Dell, 1968.

Clarke, John Henrik, ed. *American Negro Short Stories*. New York: Hill and Wang, 1967.

Cromwell, Otelia, Lorenzo D. Turner, and Eva B. Dykes, eds. *Readings from Negro Authors*. New York: Harcourt, Brace, 1931.

Cunard, Nancy, ed. *Negro Anthology*. London: Wishart, 1934.

Dreer, Herman, ed. *American Literature by Negro Authors*. New York: Macmillan, 1950.

Emanuel, James A., and Theodore Gross, eds. *Dark Symphony: Negro Literature in America*. New York: The Free Press, 1968.

Ford, Nick Aaron, and H. L. Faggett, eds. *Best Short Stories by Afro-American Writers, 1925-1950*. Boston: Meador, 1950.

Hill, Herbert, ed. *Soon, One Morning: New Writings by American Negroes, 1940-1962*. New York: Knopf, 1963.

Hughes, Langston, ed. *The Best Short Stories by Negro Writers: An Anthology from 1899 to the Present*. Boston and Toronto: Little, Brown, 1967.

Johnson, Charles S., ed. *Ebony and Topaz: A Collectanea*. New York: National Urban League, 1927.

Jones, LeRoi, and Larry Neal, eds. *Black Fire*. New York: Morrow, 1968.

Locke, Alain, ed. *The New Negro*. New York: Boni, 1925.

Watkins, Sylvester C., ed. *Anthology of American Negro Literature*. New York: Modern Library, 1944.

B. Collections of Stories by Individual Authors

Anderson, Alston. *Lover Man*. Garden City, New York: Doubleday, 1959.

Baldwin, James. *Going to Meet the Man*. New York: Dial, 1965.

Chesnutt, Charles W. *The Conjure Woman and Other Tales*. Boston: Houghton Mifflin, 1899.

_____. *The Wife of His Youth and Other Stories of The Color Line*. New York: Houghton Mifflin, 1899.

Dunbar, Paul Laurence. *Folks from Dixie*. New York: Dodd, Mead, 1898.

_____. *The Heart of Happy Hollow*. New York: Dodd, Mead, 1904.

_____. *In Old Plantation Days*. New York: Dodd, Mead, 1903.

_____. *The Strength of Gideon and Other Stories*. New York: Dodd, Mead, 1900.

Gaines, Ernest J. *Bloodline*. New York: Dial, 1968.

Hughes, Langston. *The Best of Simple*. New York: Hill and Wang, 1961.

_____. *Laughing to Keep from Crying*. New York: Holt, 1952.

_____. *Simple Speaks His Mind*. New York: Simon and Schuster, 1950.

_____. *Simple Stakes A Claim*. New York: Rinehart, 1957.

_____. *Simple Takes a Wife*. New York: Simon & Schuster, 1953.

_____. *Simple's Uncle Sam*. New York: Hill and Wang, 1965.

_____. *The Ways of White Folks*. New York: Knopf, 1934.

Jones, LeRoi. *Tales*. New York: Grove, 1967.

Kelley, William M. *Dancers on the Shore*. Garden City, New York: Doubleday, 1963.

McGirt, James E. *The Triumphs of Ephraim*. Philadelphia: McGirt, 1907.

McKay, Claude. *Gingertown*. New York: Harper, 1932.

Madden, Will A. *Five More*. New York: Exposition, 1963.

_____. *Two and One*. New York: Exposition, 1961.

Marshall, Paule. *Soul Clap Hands and Sing*. New York: Atheneum, 1961.

Toomer, Jean. *Cane*. New York: Boni & Liveright, 1923.

Walrond, Eric. *Tropic Death*. New York: Boni & Liveright, 1926.

Wright, Richard. *Eight Men*. New York: World, 1940, 1961.

_____. *Uncle Tom's Children, Five Long Stories*. New York: Harper, 1938.